Luigi Prestinenza Pu

C000255526

HyperArchitecture
Spaces in the Electronic Age

Afterword by Antonino Saggio

Birkhäuser – Publishers for Architecture
Basel • Boston • Berlin

Translation into English: Lucinda Byatt, Edinburgh

A CIP catalogue record for this book is available from the Library of Congress, Washington D.C., USA.

Deutsche Bibliothek Cataloging-in-Publication Data

Hyper architecture : spaces in the electronic age / Luigi Prestinenza Puglisi. [Transl. into Engl.: Lucinda Byatt]. - Basel ; Boston ; Berlin : Birkhäuser, 1999
ISBN 3-7643-6093-3 (Basel ...)
ISBN 0-8176-6093-3 (Boston)

Original edition:
HyperArchitettura. Spazi nell'età dell'elettronica (Universale di Architettura 38, collana diretta da Bruno Zevi; La Rivoluzione Informatica, sezione a cura di Antonino Saggio).
© 1998 Testo & Immagine, Turin

© 1999 Birkhäuser – Publishers for Architecture, P.O. Box 133, CH-4010 Basel, Switzerland.
Printed on acid-free paper produced of chlorine-free pulp. TCF ∞
Printed in Italy
ISBN 3-7643-6093-3
ISNB 0-8176-6093-3

9 8 7 6 5 4 3 2 1

Contents

My interest is in the future because I am going to spend the rest of my life there.

CHARLES F. KETTERING

1. Architecture in the age of electronics

1.1 An antecedent: the Pompidou Centre

1971. Three years after the uprisings of 1968 and two after man first landed on the moon, the designs for a new centre of art and culture commissioned by the Gaullist president, Georges Pompidou, were being examined in Paris. A total of 681 projects had been entered by architects from all over the world.

A jury had been called to examine the designs whose members included: the Dutchman Willi Sandemberg, a renowned museum expert, the Brazilian Oscar Niemeyer, who had inspired the plan for Brasilia; the American Philip Johnson, who guided architectural fashion and trends in the United States from the MoMA. The jury was chaired by the Frenchman, Jean Prouvé, an engineer, inventor and experimenter with new materials and technologies.

The competition was won, to everyone's surprise, by Renzo **8-9** Piano, Richard Rogers and Gianfranco Franchini.

The jury acted with fortunate irresponsibility. It entrusted a project with a budget equivalent to 170 billion lire, which would absorb 10% each year of the entire budget allocated to French culture, to two designers in their thirties (Rogers was 38, Piano 34) who had not yet built a major work. Above all, it was irresponsible in its architectural choice: the winning design was a transparent machine structured on slabs that could be raised and lowered to offer maximum flexibility; supported by long girders that minimised the need for pillars; all the systems were projected outwards and realized in full view so that they could be easily maintained and replaced when needed.

Lastly, the main facade included a giant screen displaying electronic messages about events in the center or cultural and political news.

The antecedents for the design for Plateau Beaubourg Centre Paris (the formal title given by the competition) include the research by Buckminster Fuller, Superstudio, and the metabolists. But above all, the English group Archigram, the source of references to macrostructures in movement and the interest in new technologies.

Six years passed between the competition and the inauguration, by which time the energetic figure of Pompidou had disappeared from the scene. Plans for the mobile floors were set aside, as they would have doubled the costs, and even the large screen on the facade was soon abandoned. In an interview given in 1993, Piano commented: the Pompidou Centre "would have been the largest TV screen in France, without having a production structure behind it."

Pompidou's successor, Giscard D'Estaing, tried to play down the avantgarde features of the structure, making it more traditional. This culminated in the intervention of Gae Aulenti who divided the floor destined for use as the Modern Art gallery into cubicles, eliminating the lightweight partitions running along tracks in the ceiling.

Renzo Piano protested placidly: "It's as if they were putting a plaster cast on a leg." Now securely launched on the international scene with several projects that were much less blatantly avantgarde, he enjoyed the success of a structure that, in spite of all the betrayals, had become the symbol of a new way of housing, producing and exhibiting culture.

The Pompidou Centre did not win the full-hearted support of the critics. For example, Kenneth Frampton attacked it by describing it as "an example of lack of wall surfaces and excessive flexibility." Alan Colquohoun accused it of populism and gigantism. Leonardo Benevolo only mentioned it briefly in his *History of Modern Architecture*. Manfredo Tafuri condemned it by talking about the technological emphasis of some young architects who "translated images that have become canons of the new natural environment into superfluous metaphors."

Reyner Banham protests: the Pompidou Centre is "the only public monument of international quality produced during the Seventies." Designed for no more than ten thousand visitors a day, it has twenty-five thousand on average, with a total of over one hundred million visitors in over twenty years. What is more, in the space of a few years, the building has become one of the most famous sights in Paris: the square in front of the Centre is a lively meeting place and the route linking Les Halles to the Pompidou Centre is the busiest pedestrian area in the city.

Richard Rogers tries to account for the success of the structure. He attributes it to the historical moment, the curiosity of a mass society with a growing interest in cultural activities, the fact that the Pompidou Centre was the first open structure dedicated to the new media. But also the spot-on artistic intuition: "The facade, he says, is like jazz, perfect in all its individual parts, but at the same time flexible and open."

The comparison deserves to be taken further. Jazz marks the break from the mechanical in favor of discontinuity, participation, spontaneity and improvisation. But also the search for fresh inspiration: for jazz players, recorded jazz is as stale as yesterday's newspaper. Furthermore, in jazz, the performance generally coincides with the composition: this means that it is alive, like conversation, and like the latter it depends on having a repertoire of available themes; breaking traditional harmony through composition by fragments, it is organized using a mosaic-type structure.

Many critics have been impressed by the Centre's imposing utility systems, by its pipes, iron, glass and the various mechanical systems. This has resulted in the preconception that it is yet another neofuturist-based eulogy to the beauty and power of the machine.

Beaubourg, however, marks the start of something new. *Firmitas*, namely attention to the values of weight and structure, is replaced by lightness, indeterminateness, transformability, the involvement of the user. We have come a long way from the logic of the "machine for living" underpinning the car, steamship or aeroplane, whose polished perfection was characteristic of industrial society products in the first half of the 20th century. Here we enter a new age, marked by electronics and characterized by three phenomena: immateriality, sensoriality, multimediality.

Immateriality is primarily expressed by transparency. Zevi – who was one of the first to realize the value of the work in Italy and made it the subject of a monograph in "Universale di architettura," the series of which he is editor – compares Beaubourg to the description of one of Italo Calvino's invisible cities: "It has no walls or ceilings and no floors: it has nothing which makes it look like a city, except for the pipes…"

It is well known that the decision to display the pipes, namely

1.1 An antecedent: the Pompidou Center

The winning design in the international competition of 1971 was a transparent machine, structured on mobile slabs and with a giant screen on the main facade showing electronic messages about events in the center or cultural and political news. Numerous changes had to be made during the construction process, annulling the initial aims and relegating them to the level of simple metaphoric statements.

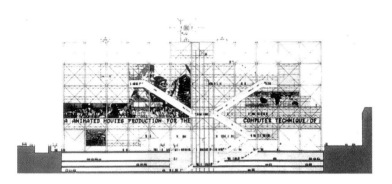

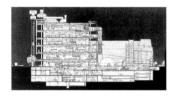

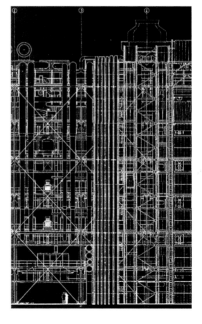

Opposite page, top: Renzo Piano, Richard Rogers, Gianfranco Franchini, Pompidou Centre (Paris, 1971-1977), main elevation. Bottom: the escalators. This page, top: the main elevation planned for the competition project; above: main section; right: detail of elevation of service facade.

the operating parts of the machine, is said to have infuriated the greatest poet of industrial technology, Mies, who sustained that this was not architecture if they were visible. The idea of visible systems in fact belongs to Archigram and the "metabolists" for whom, from the Sixties onwards, it was necessary to devaluate the traditional problems of architectural composition: they denied that the design of the facade, the rooms, the components or the details might, in themselves, in any way be central; instead, they underlined the links and relations between spaces, functions and activities in a society based on flows, many of which are immaterial.

Sensoriality is the capacity of a structure to interact with the outside world. As Rogers observes, it implies the installation of "sensitive systems which flex like the muscles in the body, minimizing the mass, shifting the forces with the help of a nervous system based on electronic impulses, sensing environmental change and recording individual requirements."

This explains the organization of the Pompidou Centre as a complex system of coordinated activities and, in overall terms, as a machine that manages information on more than one level, relating to multiple activities and using several techniques. Lastly, *multimediality* represents the choice to transform the building into an organism capable of conveying messages using various media, integrating them into the building fabric. The building becomes a screen that irradiates lights, colors and sounds and, at the same time, communicates information.

The Pompidou Centre – at least in its original design – anticipates, but without being subject to the same strong commercial pressures, Times Square and the experimental forms of 65 *electronic communication* introduced above all in Japan and the United States.

1.2 Electronic Bauhaus

1985. Eight years after the inauguration of the Pompidou Centre, Rem Koolhaas, a Dutch architect sensitive to the chaotic fascination of the contemporary metropolis, wrote an essay entitled: *The terrible beauty of the twentieth century*. It starts with these words: "Has any area in history – except perhaps the Forum in Rome – ever been richer in architectural history than the Forum des Halles and its immediate vicinity, including Beaubourg?"

The question is rhetorical and leads to a single answer: no. Because the beauty of this century lies in the mixture of activities, the intermingling of means of transport and intercommunication, the overlapping of oral, visual and audiovisual media.

In the design submitted for the Paris Library competition in 1989, Koolhaas proposed a building that played on the relationship between the solid areas of information – namely, the books – and the vacuum of the spaces for reading, meeting and interlinking, structured using the vast *vierendeel* girders explicitly taken from the Pompidou Centre. Although the project aroused considerable interest, the outcome was negative. The competition was won by the mediocre, rhetorical and antifunctional project submitted by Dominique Perrault. That same year, Rem Koolhaas won the competition for the Zentrum für Kunst und Medietechnologie (ZKM) in Karlsruhe.

12-13

OMA, the design office set up and directed by him, worked with exceptional commitment to develop the project and draw up the detailed layout.

The compulsory reference point was still the Pompidou Center, with its overlaid and integrated activities. The password is *amalgamation*: putting together a media museum, one of contemporary art, a theater, a conference room, a library, research activities and facilities for the production of music, video and virtual reality. But also the realization of an open laboratory where, like a Darwinian arena, classical art would clash with the electronic media influencing one another.

"To generate density, exploit proximity, provoke tension, maximize friction, organize in-betweens, promote filtering, sponsor identity *and* stimulate blurring," the entire program is enclosed in a single prism measuring 43 x 43 x 58 meters. Each floor contains a different activity, but they are all linked by technological spaces and distribution areas resembling large Piranesian cavities. There is a technological area in the southern part, known as the *robot* area, housing scenes from the theater, electronic equipment, projectors and other instruments that run from one floor to another as required.

2. Electronic Bauhaus

The Zentrum für Kunst und Medientechnologie in Karlsruhe designed by Rem Koolhaas can be likened to an open laboratory where, like a Darwinian arena, classical art clashes with electronic media in order to "generate density, exploit proximity, provoke tension, maximize friction, organize intermediate space, promote overlaps, sponsor identities and stimulate confusion."

Rem Koolhaas, Zentrum für Kunst und Medientechnologie (Karlsruhe, Germany, 1989). Opposite page: longitudinal section of multimedia rooms. This page, top: the eastern facade along the square opposite the entrance to the station; right: the Piranesian cavity facing the railway.

Filtered through a facade clad in polyester, the *robot*'s components can be seen from the motorway running alongside the building.

The eastern facade, which faces onto the entrance to the railway station next door, is a large screen on which films can be projected. The northern facade, which contains the vertical itineraries of the center, overlooks the railway station and, in particular, the railway tracks, creating an effect of overlying movement reminiscent of futurist aesthetics.

The media museum on the ground floor penetrates the railway station and can also be seen, through glass walls, by travelers.

With all its spatial and technical devices, the building is the prototype of a new type of multimedia center. An *electronic Bauhaus*, as Koolhaas affirms in his book S, M, L, XL.

It is worth taking this comparison a little further. Gropius' Bauhaus expresses the design method of industrial civilization: it is a factory, albeit one of ideas, a machine structured using functional standards, made to achieve set targets. Principles that acquire concrete form in a rational, lightweight, simple, dynamic construction with clear-cut geometrical foundations.

ZKM – which is a product of the electronic age – is a complex organism, based on the interaction between the various internal activities, and between these and the outside world. Its objective is to manage information, sometimes producing unexpected results. It is the flows rather than the gears that are the driving force of the 21st century. The immaterial is consequently predominant in architecture: walls lose their consistency, objects are dematerialized, the content takes over the container. Moreover, ZKM is polymorphous, both because it is in constant transformation and because every part responds to different forms of logic: the southern facade of the Centre shows its own metabolic activity, the eastern facade is transformed into a projection screen made up of rapidly moving images, the northern facade is a glass filter between two different generators of movement: one internal and vertical, the other external and horizontal.

Electronics enables any reduction to a single formal principle or compulsory standardization of the sensitive to be overcome. It manages diversity using appropriate computer programs. Unfortunately, the city council that undertook to build the center was forced to resign owing to a political scandal. The new, more conservative council preferred to abandon the ZKM project and invest in more traditional, but less controversial activities.

1.3 A library like a microchip

1992. A competition was announced in Paris for the University Library. The most interesting projects were by Rem Koolhaas 16-17 and Toyo Ito. Koolhaas presented a 64-meter high parallelepiped structure using a regular grid of pillars, whose floor slabs curved like sheets of paper until they joined together, creating a spatial *continuum* running, without a break, from the ground floor to the roof.

It is impossible to deny the references to the great projects of the history of architecture structured on the principle of rising progression. For example, the spiral in Wright's Guggenheim. But, for Koolhaas, the reference served to highlight the differences rather than to propose likenesses.

The matrix of the Guggenheim is the spiral, namely a curved three-dimensional surface, rather than prismatic volume, which for Wright was only a negative – the skyscraper or intensive luxury of Park Avenue – which he could oppose.

In the Paris Library, on the other hand, the *continuum* is created by folding the horizontal partitions that still remain within the logic of the box. The ascendant tension is created by the transformation of this flat geometry into a curve: it is the result of the partial process of mutation, whose outcome, like all incomplete mutation processes, is a hybrid. It is an object, whose intermediate form – the fact of being neither box nor spiral, but at the same time being to a certain extent both – may finally emerge, thanks to the complex calculations mastered by the computer. This proves very interesting: for example, it can be used to reason on the genesis of form or to play, inside the same manufact, on apparently irreconcilable contrasts like linear-undulating, static-dynamic, open-closed (we will come back to this point in the chapter on mutation).

Toyo Ito counters the overwhelming complexity of the space organized by Rem Koolhaas with a minimalist box: a plate

3. A LIBRARY LIKE A CHIP

The most interesting projects for the 1992 competition for the National Library in Paris were by Rem Koolhaas and Toyo Ito. Koolhaas presented a parallelepiped whose floor slabs curved like sheets of paper until they joined together, creating a spatial continuum running, without a break, from the ground floor to the roof. Toyo Ito countered this complex project with a minimalist plate formed by the juxtaposition of longitudinal bodies on two levels. The library resembles the chip in a computer: a space in which preference is given to the interconnections that transmit information. The two inner elliptical bodies suggest the thickening and contraction of energy flows.

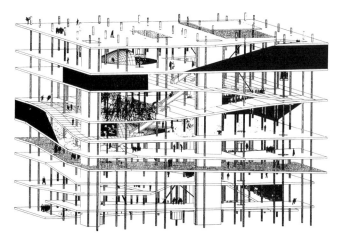

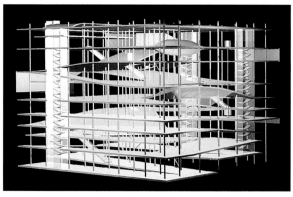

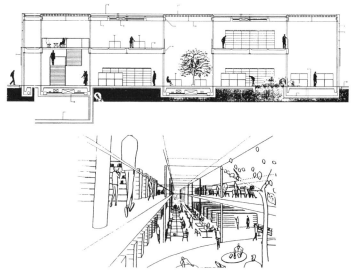

Opposite page, top: Rem Koolhaas, competition for the University Library (Paris, 1992), axonometry; bottom, rendering of the structural scheme. This page, top: Toyo Ito, competition for the University Library in Paris, model of project; center: standard cross section; bottom: interior perspective view.

formed by the juxtaposition of longitudinal bodies on two levels that face onto other longitudinal bodies of double the height; the scheme is broken in two points by elliptical bodies acting as meeting points; the outer surfaces are clad in transparent materials that allow the onlooker to glimpse the shelves and furnishings inside.

Ito rejects any expressive concession: there are no references or nods to history, allusions to consolidated language, plays on chiaroscuro or chromatic effects, outlines or harmonious modulations. As Abalos and Herreros comment in the issue of *El Croquis* dedicated to him, Ito continues his search for an absolute form of simplicity, "a new simplicity that believes that complexity cannot be expressed in geometric terms, or to be more precise, that geometric complexity and its deformations have ceased to be pertinent responses to architectural expression." The architectural ideal is therefore to search for a neutral, homogeneous, aperspective space, so transparent that it is ephemeral.

"My project," states Ito, "is the antithesis of monumental architecture, buildings that want to live for eternity."

The precarious and inexpressive nature of the shell shifts the onlooker's attention from the container to the content. With the result that the library resembles the chip in a computer: both are aseptic spaces which give preference to the interconnections that enable the transmission of information and both are structured round a grid of itineraries, preferably straight and, at all events, based on the logic of the shortest journey.

Moreover, the two elliptical bodies included in the design, although they have no immediate counterpart in real computer architecture, namely, that of the microchip, suggest the movement of energy flows: "The oval," Ito observes, "gives fluidity to the structure, fosters its openness to the outside and its interaction with its surroundings, exactly like an eddy in the water interacts with neighboring currents."

1.4 Waves in the sea of communication

1991. A year before the competition for the University Library in Paris, Toyo Ito had taken part in the London exhibition entitled *Visions of Japan*, setting up a room which he

entitled *Simulation*, but which, on Arata Isozaki's advice, he
then called by a more popular name: *Dreams*. ₂₀
The room measured 10 x 28 meters. It was fitted with a float-
ing floor coated in matte acrylic panels onto which twenty-six
projectors hanging from the ceiling were projecting images of
Tokyo. A liquid crystal screen was mounted on the short wall;
the longer one consisted of a slightly undulating wall clad in
aluminium panels hidden by a curtain, onto which forty-four
projectors threw other images of the Japanese capital. Lastly,
a battery of amplifiers diffused music through the building,
processed by a tuner, taken from the sounds of the city.
Toyo Ito commented, with amusement, that at the inauguration the Prince of Japan had to drink a cup of *sakè* before
entering a space that was both so chaotic and so evanescent,
and that Prince Charles – a sworn enemy of the metropolis –
asked what messages were hidden behind the images. When
Ito replied that perhaps there was nothing behind the images,
he asked him whether he was an incurable optimist.
In his works, Ito often works on an image drained of all meaning, almost left in an impressionist state, a stage that has
reached the senses but has not yet made a formal impression
on the intellect. Like *Egg of Wind*, a sculpture-kaleidoscope ₂₀
clad in drilled aluminium panels that reflects the images of the
city projected onto it and, at the same time, reveals others from
the TVs placed inside it. Exactly like those of a television when
the sound is turned off, the images lose all meaning, becoming
purely sensorial phenomena: colours and shapes that vibrate
and fluctuate in space. Seen from this perspective, space no
longer appears to be a vacuum in which solid bodies live, but
rather a medium through which information is diffused.
Let us go back to Ito's comment in which he told Prince Charles
that the images could not hide anything. This might well have
been said by Andy Warhol, with whom Ito certainly shared a
fascination for reality as manifested through happenings, leav-
ing aside any contextualization or conceptual mediation.
But whereas Warhol freezes the image into figures with clearly defined outlines (whether they are the can of Campbell's
soup or the portraits of Marilyn, Jackie or Mao Tse-tung), Ito
captures it when it is still a flow of energy. Electronics, he later

4. WAVES IN THE SEA OF COMMUNICATION

Ito often works on an image drained of all meaning, almost reduced to an impressionist state, a stage that has reached the senses but has not yet made a formal impression on the intellect and in which space no longer appears to be a vacuum in which solid bodies live, but rather a medium through which information is diffused.

Opposite page, top: Toyo Ito, The Dreams *room at the exhibition* Visions of Japan *(London, 1991-92); bottom,* Egg of Wind *(Okawabata River City, 1988-91). This page:* Wind Tower *(Yokohama, 1986).*

wrote in an essay in 1997, is like a sea, like the waves, like a breath of life. We live in an age that has overcome mechanism, but has not yet changed the functional – and therefore, in a sense, mechanistic – organization of homes: "We have not yet found," Ito affirms, "a space that reflects the idea of living in the age of electronics".

Yet electronics has overturned the formal coordinates of the environment in which we live. You need only think of car design, Ito points out. The Citröen Deux Chevaux and the Volkswagen Beetle have given way to the modern Japanese models of Toyota and Nissan, whose forms no longer reflect their inner mechanisms but more abstract processes: easy, comfortable driving, the recognition and management of controls, automatic position control, radio and telephone contacts, climate control, ergonomics, energy saving, automated safety mechanisms. The changes in other sectors are even more far-reaching: one need only think of fields like bioengineering that require the collaboration of biology and microelectronics.

What will the electronic house look like? It will certainly be different from early 20th century homes, namely, the small villa with a sloping roof, garden, a kitchen laid out according to the principles of *Existenzminimum*, a dining room with chrome furniture. And also from the most modern electric house, designed to optimize the use of electrical household appliances in order to minimize the burden of housework for working women.

In 1989, following the *PAO 2* installation: *"Dwelling for Tokyo Nomad Woman,"* Toyo Ito attempted to give a form to the electronic house. He made an egg-shaped tent, surrounded by transparent veils. Inside are three almost evanescent pieces of furniture: one for make-up, one for eating, one for intellectual activities. It is very different from the traditional house: the latter is rooted in the ground and filled with objects with symbolic or functional value, it represents a world apart, almost a microcosm; it is exactly the opposite of the electronic house which is, by definition, unstable and not self-sufficient.

Electronics stimulates nomadism, namely, the willingness to be uprooted from places, to live traveling, both in a physical sense (in a car, train, plane) and using communications instruments (radio, television, Internet, telephone, teleconference). Moreover, it is not autarchic by nature and presupposes the management of complexity through joint effort, the union of many resources and forms of intelligence. Lastly, by accelerating the exchange of goods and making them available everywhere, electronics eliminates the need for their domestic storage.

Toyo Ito bases his remarks on the central role played in an electronic society by the sense of feeling and the importance of skin on the arguments put forward by Marshall McLuhan, the brilliant Canadian media expert. By skin, he means a sensitive epidermis that covers buildings and enables the domestic environment to interact with the urban space, absorbing lights, sounds, flows and returning images and vital tensions to the outside.

But if, Toyo Ito adds, the house must be soft and flexible and not rigid and dense, it will be conceived as an electronic garment that allows people to live the virtual nature of the metropolis, becoming "Tarzans in the media forest." Fascinated by nature, Ito thinks of electronics as energy able to reintegrate man in the environment, in the flow of life.

Already in 1986, in Yokohama, he designed an organism that was both natural and artificial: the *Wind Tower* is a structure 21 that filters the air, sounds and noises of the city, transforming them into light. The result is an architectonic object rooted on the spot, absolutely contextual but subject to change, because the air, light and sounds around it are never the same.

In 1997 Ito completed his masterpiece: the media library in Sendai. He designed a 7-story building measuring 50 x 50 x 30 24-25 meters, each of whose floors would be dedicated to a different activity. The floors are connected using pylons as light as bamboo canes. In the center of each pylon is a hole which – crossing through the building from sky to earth – captures the rays of the sun above, the dampness from below and serves to duct the vertical connection elements and electronic cabling.

The media library appears to be immersed in fluid: water, light, information and the floors supported by lightweight pylon supports make it vibrate. When illustrating the project, Ito mentions the primordial elements, the philosophers Laotzu (4th century B.C.) and Kumazawa (12th century A.D.). The conclusion, which may not be approved of by the more rigorous cybernetic experts, certainly has an outstanding poet-

5. FLUIDS

In 1997 Ito designed the media library in Sendai whose floors were connected using pylons as light as bamboo canes. In the center of each pylon was a hole which – crossing through the building from sky to

earth – captured the rays of the sun above, the dampness from below and ducted the vertical connection elements and IT cabling. The media library appears to be immersed in fluid: water, light, information.

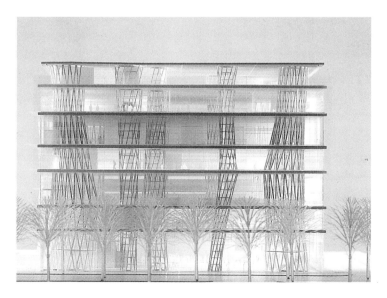

Opposite page: Toyo Ito, media library (Sendai, Japan, 1997, in the process of completion), model. This page, top: conceptual drawing; bottom: facade of building.

ic value: the essence of the media forest lies in the very old principle of becoming.

1.5 Mies + Futurism

If Beaubourg is the building that prefigures the age of electronics, the acknowledged master of the new designers is Mies.

Koolhaas admires him to the point of plagiarising him in his design for the Morgan Bank in Amsterdam and the patio houses in Rotterdam. He is attracted by Mies' use of transparency and the reduction of architecture to a *virtual nothingness*.

Toyo Ito also dedicated a number of written works to Mies and, in particular, the first part of the essay entitled *Tarzans in the media forest* in which he affirms that the antecedent for the media library in Sendai and the Tower of the Winds is the Barcelona Pavilion, a fluid architecture whose vibrating and mobile storys are reflected in the two swimming pools: "The transparency of the Barcelona Pavilion is not like that of clear air. It feels as if we are deep in water looking at things, and it may well be described as translucent. The infinite fluidity felt in the pavilion must arise from this translucent liquid-like space."

Mies also provides the inspiration for another protagonist of the age of electronics: Zaha Hadid. The fire station on the Vitra
28 campus in Weil Am Rhein, focused on the deconstruction of volumes into dividing plates, is reminiscent of the Barcelona pavilion. With the difference that here the dynamism of the forms directed into space takes the place of the albeit unstable neoplastic equilibrium; as has been observed, the building gives formal expression to the vibrating alarm signal calling the firemen on duty.

Hadid's drawings of the Vitra fire station show the close relationship between them and the architecture. And not only because computer-assisted design allows the complexity of the moving forms to be accurately represented, but also because the static and formally defined plans, elevations and traditional perspective views are replaced by elaborate drawings of quivering forms and overlaid planes seen from unusual and antinaturalistic viewpoints – almost autonomous works that resemble the avantgarde paintings of the early 20th century.
29 Hadid's projects expressly reflect Suprematism and Malevich's

works, but also the early period of Duchamp. Less evident but equally undeniable is the debt of the American architect Eisenman to Futurism, both in the Guardiola house in Cadiz, a residence built on the alternating movement of the sea along the beach, and the Architecture Faculty of the University of Cincinnati, stemming from a dual undulating movement: the geometric shape of the old building and the vibrating new curvilinear building.

"The origin can be traced back to the Italian futurist, Giacomo Balla (*Dinamismo di un cane al guinzaglio*, 1911), but the universally well known image is Marcel Duchamp's *Nude descending the stairs* (1912-16). You will remember the image: a series of superimposed images of the figure, like a photo taken using too long an exposure, in which the individual movements overlap one another […] It is an extraordinarily interesting technique that has remained unchanged for eighty years in architecture […]." **29**

If Eisenman follows the example of Balla and Duchamp, Gehry is indebted to Boccioni. The volumes of the Disney auditorium in Los Angeles or the Guggenheim Museum in Bilbao visualize the movement of the notes in a symphony, but also the plastic dynamism of *The City Rises*. There is also something vaguely Boccionesque about Daniel Libeskind's recent masterpiece, the design for the new extension of the Victoria & Albert Museum, where the rotation of a wall around a spiral creates a whirling and vertiginous volume that would have delighted the author of *Stati d'animo*, but which would be almost impossible to control in architecture without the aid of the computer. **32-33** **73**

We need go no further. These formal similarities with Futurism may be useful to help us understand that, through electronics, architecture has also rediscovered ancient expressive desires – whose properties have not yet been fully explored – suppressed by the advent of the rigid and trivializing *koinè* of International Style. But these may also deviate us from the historic specificity of events; in particular, they distract us from the fact that, whereas Futurism is the art of the electric age, namely, the car and household electrical appliances, the new architecture is the art of the electronic age, namely, the computer and information

6. A MODERN TRADITION

The static and formally defined plans, elevations and traditional perspective views are replaced by elaborate drawings of penetrating forms and overlaid planes seen from unusual and antinaturalistic viewpoints, that resemble the avantgarde paintings of the early 20th century.

Opposite page: drawing by Zaha Hadid showing the fire station on the Vitra Campus (Weil am Rhein, Germany, 1990-93). This page: Marcel Duchamp, Nu descendant un escalier, no. 2 *(1912).*

sciences. And electronics is characterized by three keywords: *projection, mutation, simulation*.

2. Projection

2.1 An antecedent: Duchamp

The dictionary gives the following definition of the term *project*: "1. Jut out or protrude, cast; 2. Cause to fall on a screen." For architects, the term *project* is linked to descriptive geometry: orthogonal projections, axonometry, perspective. For the philosopher, it means reflection: to project our thoughts onto an ideal mirror in order to observe their structure and inner consistency with sufficient detachment. For the psychoanalyst, it means *transference*, namely the need to project oneself into another person, in order to acquire a better understanding of an aspect of ourselves that would otherwise elude us. For the scientist, projection means the construction of models. A model reflects reality and its accuracy depends on the accuracy with which each property of the model reproduces the object studied. Lastly, for the artist, projection is the foundation of representation, whether figurative or abstract. If art and reality are in any way related, this relationship can only be achieved using projections.

Marcel Duchamp realized this when, on 8 August 1913, he moved into his new studio in Rue Saint-Hippolyte in Paris and **34-35** started to outline the general framework of *La mariée mise a nu par ses célibataires, même* (which could be translated as *The Bride Stripped Bare by her Bachelors, Even*, except that by doing so we lose the countless double meanings and plays on words that for years have been the subject of the critics' increasingly deconstructed exegesis). He continued to elaborate this work, which is also known as *The Large Glass*, for the rest of his life and it contains most of his research.

The Large Glass is somewhat similar to Joyce's *Ulysses*: a fascinating work with a plurality of meanings, but at the same time abstruse, hermetic and often indecipherable.

The first and most obvious meanings of the work are surrealistic: *The Large Glass* symbolizes the ascension of a bride to heaven (the Virgin of the Christian tradition? the female concept?), while on the earth, below the line of the horizon, she is the object of her suitors' desire, namely nine human types represented by the same number of alchemistic molds (malic molds) who have undressed her (in short, the horizon represents the bride's dress).

Alongside the nine malic moulds, a sledge and a chocolate grinder, which represent the principle of energy production, provide the ideal motor for the composition.

Proceeding with his usual exasperating and vague slowness, Duchamp decides to link the nine malic molds to each other using wires that are one meter long and which, in turn, represent the pipes used to transmit the life-giving principle (pure energy? light? gas? libido? – the critics also disagree on this point).

For this purpose, having exhausted Puteaux's discussions on mathematics, measurements and the fourth dimension, he uses a rigorous geometric procedure, albeit in its surrealistic paradoxical nature: he links the nine malic molds with meter-long wires, but whose rounded form is obtained by creating a deformation of the straight unit of measurement.

Duchamp writes, "If a straight, horizontal wire, one meter in length, falls from a height of one meter onto a horizontal plane deforming itself at will, it will produce a new figure of unit of length." Duchamp performs the operation three times. He obtains three different forms of unit of measurement, no longer straight but curvilinear: three of the infinite forms determined by chance; he calls them *3 stoppages étalon*.

Using each of the *3 stoppages étalon* three times, he draws nine itineraries on the canvas, each of which is one metre long, but each is laid out using its own individual geometry.

It is evident that there is something more than a simple symbolic construction (a banal allegory of the relationship between the rule and the case or the unity that links human types…). But in order to understand the meaning, we must look for an interpretative key outside *The Large Glass*. For example, in two works also by Duchamp.

The first is entitled *3 stoppages étalon* and consists of a box 36 containing three glass rulers, onto which three curved wires are stuck, and the same number of wooden rulers, whose

7. THE CITY RISES

If Zaha Hadid follows the example of Duchamp, Gehry is indebted to Boccioni. The volumes of his compositions visualize the movement of the notes in a symphony, but also the plastic dynamism of The City Rises.

Frank Owen Gehry, Guggenheim Museum (Bilbao, 1991-1997).

34

8. Projections

The Large Glass symbolizes the ascension of a bride to heaven, while on earth, below the line of the horizon, she is the object of her suitors' desire, namely nine human types represented by the same number of alchemistic molds (malic molds) who have undressed her. Alongside the nine malic molds, a sledge and a chocolate grinder, which represent the main producer of energy and provide the ideal motor for the composition. The 3 stop-pages étalon are one-meter-long straight wires that fall from a height of one meter and are deformed by landing on a horizontal plane. The three different forms are three of the possible infinite forms – not rectilinear, but curvilinear – of the unit of measure determined by chance. Il Réseaux des stoppages étalon *is a canvas with nine itineraries created by using each of the three curved meters three times: nine itineraries each one meter long, each laid out using its own individual geometry.*

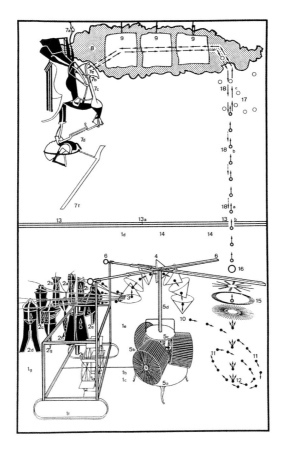

Headed arrows:
route of the illuminating gas

Straight arrows:
language of the bride

Key to the elements in The Large Glass: 1. Sleigh; 1a. Water mill; 1c. Trap door to the basement; 1d. Pulley; 1e. Revolution of the Bénédictine bottle; 1f. Runners; 2. Cemetery of uniforms and liveries; 2a. Priest; 2b. Delivery boy; 2c. Gendarme; 2d. Cavalryman; 2e. Policeman; 2f. Undertaker; 2g. Lackey; 2h. Errand boy; 2i. Station master; 3. Capillary tubes; 4. Sieves; 5. Chocolate grinder; 5a. Louis XV chassis; 5b. Rollers; 5c. Tie; 5d. Bayonet; 6. Scissors; 7. Bride; 7a. Suspension ring of the hanging woman; 7b. Mortice joint; 7c. Stem; 7d. Wasp; 7e. Head or eyes; 8. Flesh-colored Milky Way; 9. Draught pistons; 10. Ventilator-churn; 11. Toboggan Sliding or slopes; 12. 3 crash-splashes; 13 Horizon – bride's dress; 13a. Vanishing point of the bachelor perspective; 13b. Prism with Lincoln-Wilson effect and 9 holes; 14. Boxing match; 15. Oculist witnesses; 16. Kodak lens; 17. 9 shots; 18. Handler of gravity; 18a. Tripod; 18b. Rod; 18c. Black ball.

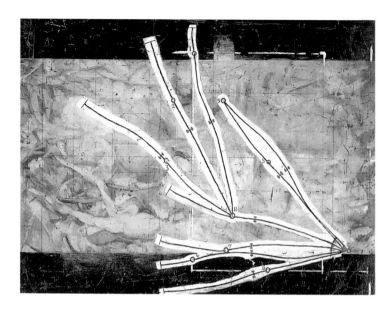

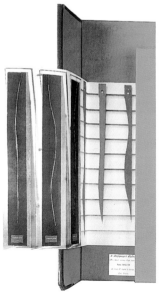

Top: Marcel Duchamp, Réseaux des stoppages étalon. *Left: M. Duchamp,* 3 stoppages étalon *(1913-14). Above: Joseph Kosuth,* One and three chairs *(1965).*

Peter Eisenman, schemes, House VI *(Cornwall, Connecticut, 1972-75).*

curvilinear shape matches those of the wires glued onto the glass rulers.

36 The second is entitled *Réseaux des stoppages étalon*, a canvas with nine itineraries created by using each of the three curved meters three times.

The two works – *3 stoppages étalon* and *Réseaux des stoppages étalon* – are closely interconnected. Four distinct transformations of the same object can clearly be seen in both.

The first transformation – from the straight wire to the curved wire – is *anamorphosis*. In scientific terms, it could be described as the projection, within defined spatial conditions and using pre-established operations, of a rectilinear series of points in an homologous curve.

The second transformation – from the curved wire to the curved wooden meter – entails the transition from the single-dimensional reality of the wire to the three-dimensional reality of the support. This is achieved using a projection, even if it is simpler than the previous one, because it involves a straight-forward translation and superimposition.

The third transformation – from the curved wooden meter to the image of the curve on the canvas – again involves a translation and superimposition, but also entails a reduction in the size of the object represented: from three to two dimensions.

The fourth transformation – from an image showing exclusively its own contents to an image that is enriched by the contents of other works – occurs through the comparison and projection of meanings.

By projecting the meanings of one work onto another, it is right to think that the *stoppages étalon* symbolize an energy transmission network, just like *The Large Glass*. But, vice versa, we could also project the meanings of the *stoppages étalon* onto *The Large Glass*, hypothesizing that the latter is a conceptual study focused on the concept of transformation through projective permutations.

Let us stop here.

2.2 Projection and conceptual art

What does Duchamp show us? At least four things.

First: we can realize works of art that explore the mechanisms of conceptualization and representation in which the aesthetic value of what is represented is secondary. The *stoppages étalon* reject any appreciation relating to their form, composition, color, or beauty, because they are not pertinent.

Second: the objects themselves, emptied of all aesthetic value, become transparent: they are only valuable as markers of the operations carried out on them. Our attention is shifted from the object to the relationships between objects.

Third: in order to make the onlooker understand that the discussion is focused on a metadiscussion and not on representation, contrary to traditional art which embraces by involving the senses, the work of art must produce a feeling of estrangement. This results in the expedient of presenting works that question the boundary between what is representation and what is reality (what is the real unit of measurement? The abstract concept of measurement, the wire of a meter, the curvilinear rigid meter or its representation on canvas?), playing on the double meanings that produce a short-circuit in meaning (is a curved meter a meter?) and, lastly, using commonplace objects of limited denotative and connotative value (before Duchamp, did anyone ever think of using such a banal object as a meter in a work of art?).

Fourth: to pass from one medium of representation to another – for example, from a 2D to a 3D reality or from the latter to the conceptual reality – it is essential to use projections, whether these are anamorphoses, translations or even metaphors.

Duchamp was regarded by many critics as the precursor of conceptual art, which developed in the second half of the Sixties. There are numerous affinities between Duchamp's ready-mades and the tautologies of Atkinson, Baldwin, Bochner, Burn, Darboven, Graham, Ramsden, and Venet. One work in particular recalls the projections of the *3 stoppages étalon*. It is *One and three chairs* by Joseph Kosuth: a composition consist- 36 ing of a real chair, a life-size photographic reproduction and the definition of a chair taken from a dictionary.

By choosing a commonplace object and multiplying it by three, Kosuth removes any iconic value, with the result that its meaning no longer lies in the object itself as it is immediately perceived but in the correlation of signs, the series of linguistic and extralinguistic associations to which the work alludes. The chair is therefore an object because it is also an image and concept for us. Moreover, it is an image because it is both concept and object.

Conclusion: art, like reality, is based on a series of projective relations, in a game of reflections, each of which permits the representation of the object, but alone can never succeed in exhausting its content.

But if knowledge and art take part in an unending game of projections, there can be no difference in principle between conceptualization and metaphorization. In fact, metaphor, like concept, lives in the projective space, given that it is a figure based on homology, similarity, the interchange between one reality and another analogous or assimilable reality. The photographed chair, the chair-object and the chair-word are, in other words, metaphors of each other.

Marshall McLuhan reached a similar conclusion when, in the Sixties, he tackled the study of the media, namely the instruments used to convey messages. The latter enable reality to be articulated and structured in a metaphoric continuum. The same object, translated from one medium to another, is clarified, but also assumes new connotations and interpretative openings.

Exactly like the wire in *3 stoppages étalon*, as it passes from one medium to another, it becomes a unit of measurement, then a spatial grid and lastly a conductor of magical energy. Or, like *One and three chairs* in the dimensions of space, image and writing.

2.3 Verdussen of Utrecht

Of course, not all metaphors are equally significant. Borges and Casares, the authors of *Chronicles of Bustos Domenq*, make fun of artists who lose themselves in a world where they cannot recognise the boundaries between reality and fiction, distracted by the play of mirrors in what has become over-subtle conceptualisation.

They resemble the poet Urbas who takes part in a competition on the theme of the rose and overcomes his adversaries, winning a prize of five hundred thousand pesos, because he presents a rose (what is more poetic than the truth? And truer than the truth?).

The poet Urbas, who annihilates poetry, being unable to find a more perfect projection than that of the object on itself, is flanked by the architect Verdussen of Utrecht. The latter adopts an even more radical position, because – since he uses non-figurative art – unlike Urbas, he cannot use the object instead of its own representation, and namely, cannot escape the confines of art by presenting the real object.

Verdussen must therefore affirm that architecture is the projection of itself because architecture is allergic to any heteronomous commingling based exclusively on the logic of the composition of its own constituent parts: wall, windows, doors, floors and roof. This results in the need to plan a composition whose motivations lie within the play itself.

This is how Borges and Casares describe the uninhabitable masterpiece realised by the extremely learned Dutch architect:

> The building [...] occupies a rectangular site, measuring six metres by barely eighteen. Each of the six doors on the ground floor façade communicates, with a gap of ninety centimetres, with another identical single opening door, and so on until there are a total of sixteen doors. From the balconies of the house opposite, the academic can see that the first floor is full of six-step stairs which lead up and down in zig-zags; the second consists of just windows; the third, thresholds; the fourth and top floor, of floors and ceilings. The building is made from glass, a detail that makes it particularly easy to examine from the neighbouring houses. This gem is so perfect that no one has dared to imitate it.

The target of Borges and Casares' irony is almost certainly Le Corbusier, to whom the book is co-dedicated ("To these three great forgotten figures: Picasso, Joyce, Le Corbusier"), but a modern-day reader can hardly avoid associating the description with the Five Architects and, in particular, Eisenman's *House VI*.

2.4 Eisenman Verdussen

Designed and built in 1972-75, the house aroused considerable **44-45** interest. Even now, at a distance of twenty-five years, it continues to be controversial (Bill Hubbard Jr., *Harvard Design Magazine*, no. 2, 1997: "The house that sends you into ecstasies or drives you up the wall.")

House VI is a weekend house of modest dimensions: a living room and kitchen-dining room on the ground floor, and a bathroom and bedroom on the first floor.

From a composition point of view, it complies with stringent geometrical laws. However, as Eisenman himself affirms: "It is not rationality that has shaped these spaces; they are determined by a formal system that has been chosen and manipulated arbitrarily."

[37] Some of Eisenman's drawings show, albeit without any clear demonstration, that the whole house, inserted into a cube, is structured using cube-shaped submodules. The dominant formal motif is therefore the manipulation of the squares that generate the ground plans and walls of the living room, bedroom and adjoining spaces. There is also a game of slipping and forward movement: for example, the living room compared to the bedroom overhead and the bathroom compared to the kitchen below. Then there are the large transverse planes: cutting the house into four, helping to define spaces that would otherwise be lost in the fragmentation of cuts and slipping.

Then there are the harmonies between solid and empty spaces, between void and void, full and full, between the stair and the pseudo-stair (namely a stair that only works if the house is turned upside down). Lastly, there are the colors used to highlight the individual floors.

This evokes a certain similarity with the neoplastic compositions. However, the latter, in particular the Schröder residence in Rietveld, use floors and colors that explode the box and give dynamism to the space along strength-axes. In *House VI*, on the other hand, the masonry fragments appear to dialogue with each other in an attempt to recompose the volumes recently called into question.

This sensation is confirmed by the internal spaces. The solids and the voids of the walls are joined to those of the walls opposite using visual harmonies, emphasized by lines running along the ceiling or floor, or by strategically positioned structural elements.

Born from an abstract play on planes and volumes, the house is barely habitable. Eisenman, for example, compelled the owners to divide the double bed in half to accommodate a cut in the floor, the projection of an equivalent line in the ceiling. He ignored the need for a dining area, with a pillar standing in the center ("The column as uninvited guest at the dining room table," observed a commentator.) The estimate of $ 35,000 tripled to a final bill of $ 100,000. He opposed the idea of adding a comfortable second floor until Arthur Drexler and Colin Rowe intervened to petition for one. He obliged the owners to send their young daughter away on the occasion of Philip Johnson's visit. He also compelled them to have the house redecorated by Massimo Vignelli before photographs were taken.

Eisenman theorises about the misanthropic nature of the house using paradoxical reasoning: habitability is to space as representation is to a picture. Habitability prompts the observer to take immediate possession, to enjoy its perceptive and symbolic values, but not to make enquiries regarding the structure of the work. This gives rise to the need for coldness, indifference to the functions, distance: architecture, just like a conceptual work of art must produce estrangement.

William Gass sustains: The most comfortable objects are the most tyrannical, because we need them to be obedient and they distract us from thinking. *House VI*, constructed to obey a single formal manipulation, allows an intricate intertwining of surfaces, spaces and lines and "provides a playground for the absolute mind."

Lay religion and aesthetic asceticism: Eisenman is a formal terrorist, a priest of limits and excess. Let us return to the concept of projection. Eisenman calls his first works *cardboard houses*. He wishes to underline their virtual character, but also the uninfluential role of their effective realization. In principle, they could be drawn on paper without losing any of their conceptual interest, which is reduced to a game of projections that could be managed perfectly well by descriptive geometry. Compared to real construction, paper allows an absolute dematerialization of the object. And, having been rendered transparent, the building would resemble the works designed by con-

44

9. EISENMAN VERDUSSEN

Eisenman shuns welcoming houses. Habitability is to space as representation is to a picture. Habitability prompts the observer to take immediate possession, to enjoy its perceptive and symbolic values, but not to make enquiries regarding the structure of the work. This gives rise to the need for coldness, indifference to the functions, distance: architecture, just like a conceptual work of art must produce estrangement. William Gass sustains: The most comfortable objects are the most tyrannical, because we need them to be obedient and they distract us from thinking. House VI, *constructed to obey a single formal manipulation, allows an intricate intertwining of surfaces, spaces and lines and "provides a playground for the absolute mind."*

Peter Eisenman, House VI *(Cornwall, Connecticut, 1972-75): above, detail of the stair. Opposite page, top: view of the house from the west; bottom right: living room; left, first and second floor plans.*

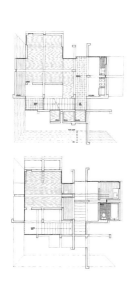

ceptual artists at the same period (Kosuth, Sol Lewitt, etc.), not to be built but merely represented using diagrams and drawings, or described in formal reports.

But what happens if the projection on which the representation is based is, in turn, projected on itself?

Eisenman tries to answer this question in *House X*. He built an axonometric model of the house and applied to a 3D medium rules such as axonometric projections that were only valid for a 2D medium.

Result: the model looks deformed. To be seen without distortions, it can only be looked at from a squint point of view, the only one that makes the slanting walls look straight. This produces the paradox that the axonometry, which would not normally require a special point of view, when applied to an unusual medium becomes a sort of perspective which, instead, presupposes one.

The projection is therefore no longer a faithful (or, better: taken for granted, unproblematic) representation of the object and becomes anamorphosis. Anamorphosis opens the horizons of a non-Euclidean topological space based on homeomorphism, namely, on the properties that remain unchanged when an object is deformed.

Then, if – as occurs in the topological universe – a lozenge becomes a rectangle and a triangle can change into a circle, similarity becomes a problem. In the same way as the flow of similarities was a problem during the projections of Duchamp's *3 stoppages étalon*.

2.5 Architecture of silence

Let us now hypothesize that there is a correspondence between architectural language and verbal language. If architectonic elements correspond to words and composition rules to syntax, Eisenman constructs a language without words; an architecture of silence and transparency; language reduced to pure form where, as Gandelsonas already noted, the semantic dimension is paralyzed and syntax assumes unlimited importance.

The architecture of silence undoubtedly finds a precedent in Loos, whom Eisenman cites on numerous occasions. He is attracted, among other things, by Loos' reduction of architecture to a quality-less object (or better: pretends to reduce architecture to a quality-less object).

But a more interesting precedent may be found in Ludwig Wittgenstein's architecture, the philosopher of language whose *Tractatus logico-philosophicus* classified symbolic logic, namely, the technique of calculation that forms the basis of computer logic.

We are in 1926. Wittgenstein's sister, Margaret Stonborough – who had just commissioned Paul Engelmann to build her a house – decided to involve her brother in the building process. **48-49** Ludwig had an innate propensity for architecture: in 1914 he had helped his friend Eccles to furnish his house; he designed nearly all the furniture for his flat in Cambridge and, lastly, he designed the mountain farm to which he withdrew in Norway.

Having just got over a nervous breakdown, Ludwig enjoyed his work with Engelmann. His old acquaintance and their shared passion for Loos' architecture, of whom one was a disciple and the other an admirer, guaranteed a formal ground for agreement. However, Ludwig soon set Engelmann aside, becoming in practice the sole person responsible for his sister's house.

He made very few alterations to Engelmann's original project: the volumetric layout was left unchanged, if we exclude the small entrance block; he made a few minor modifications to the size of the windows and their reciprocal positions; he accepted the internal layout, except for one or two minimal changes to the partitions.

However, these imperceptible modifications represented an enormous drain on Ludwig's energies, as well as calling for an enormous intellectual effort. In fact, after a day on the site, he confessed that he felt exhausted. Every question, even the most banal, prompted painstaking analysis. When a blacksmith asked him whether a millimeter was important, he replied, in his frighteningly loud voice, that even half a millimeter was essential.

Wittgenstein's exasperated attention to the smallest details can only be explained by his absolute need for rigor: every deviation, imperfection or shift away from the exact form ran the risk of classifying the object at the extreme limit of poor construction or in the abyss of ornamentation, or fatuousness.

48

10. Silence and trasparency

Although he appreciated the reductive work Loos had accomplished, Wittgenstein criticized Loos for filling his own architecture with eternal values. He guessed that the simplicity and bare proportions of modern architecture hid an even more serious crime than that identified by Loos in ornamentation. Wittgenstein's ideal is "a certain degree of coldness. A temple to house passions, without interfering with them," a house that contains life, but has nothing to do with it. Architectonic objects, like facts must be purified of all subjective connotation and reduced to their simple denotative value; architectonic space, like symbolic logic must become a transparent building that contains facts, composing them but not altering or modifying them.

Opposite page: Paul Engelmann and Ludwig Wittgenstein, house for Margaret Stonborough (Vienna, 1926-1928), entrance facade. This page, top: southern side; bottom, left: eastern side, right, ground floor plan, first version (November 1926).

This leads to a sort of contradiction that has trapped many critics: on the one hand, Wittgenstein dedicated the utmost attention to shape, dimensions and proportions and, on the other, he obstinately refused any rules established *a priori*.

Although the esegetists have endeavoured to discover the proportions of this building, nothing has been found.

Those that have been found show approximations of five or more per cent; they are therefore too imprecise to have been used by an eternally dissatisfied character who did not think twice before demolishing, once the work had been finished, the living room ceiling in order to raise it three centimeters and who, the day the windows were fitted, compelled poor Margaret Respinger – who was more interested in the architect than in the architecture – to spend hours opening and shutting them to check that they were perfectly perpendicular. Moreover, Wittgenstein spent much of his energy on breaking symmetries (e.g., eliminating one of the two niches in the library), breaking up alignments (e.g., positioning the entrance door out of line compared to the windows above), differentiating and disarticulating the parts (e.g., designing different windows for each facade).

Such a total rejection of pre-established formal systems can only be explained by the fact that, for a philosopher like Wittgenstein, who was radically linked to the pure essentiality of facts, every aprioristic conception is too imbued with connotative values, metaphysical references, to be satisfactory.

In fact, although Wittgenstein appreciated the reductive work accomplished by Loos, he criticized Loos for filling his architecture with eternal values, a fact that he denied in words. He guessed that the simplicity and bare proportions of modern architecture hid an even more serious crime than that identified by Loos in the form of ornamentation. These houses – he argued on the occasion of the Wiener Werkbund exhibition of 1932 – look at you as if to say "look how pretty I am."

Wittgenstein affirms: "My ideal is a certain degree of coldness. A temple to house passions, without interfering with them."

We can translate this as a house that contains life, but has nothing to do with it (incidentally, it is worth noting the parallel with Eisenman's *House VI*).

If we replace the term "architectonic object" with the word "fact," and the term "space" with the word "logic," we arrive at the philosophy of *Tractatus*: facts, like architectonic objects, must be purified of all subjective connotation and reduced to their simple denotative value; whereas logic, like architectonic space, must become a transparent building that contains facts, composing them but not altering or modifying them. Logic is in fact pure tautology, which can be organized according to mathematical procedures – projections, we might be tempted to say – that are the best instrument available to scientific activity precisely because they add nothing and remove nothing from reality, but simply translate it. This rigorously analytical construction is in fact the end point of Wittgenstein's ascetic and mystical vision, one which is very close to that of Eisenman: transparency not only represents the maximum effort made to conceptualize the sayable, but also the only window through which we are allowed to glimpse the unsayable: "I am not interested – Wittgenstein would later affirm – in erecting a building, rather than seeing, before me, the transparent foundations of possible buildings"; in other words, in short, the structure of the world (my world).

3. Mutation

3.1 Transformations

Let us go back to the 17th century, and more precisely to Bacon. He tells us that "it is an excellent invention according to which Pan, namely the world, chose Echo as his wife (in preference to all other voices) because true philosophy faithfully reproduces the world's own words." We can translate this as follows: knowledge has always been a process of constant clarification that occurs through reflections, refractions, translations that let us glimpse the world through their transparency. But while the game of projections has always fascinated philosophers and scientists, research into language has become a central, at times obsessive, theme since the early 20th century. Formal logic, structuralism, set theory, hermeneutics: the study of contents is replaced by the analysis of relations.

52

11. Dematerialized Architecture

Form is dematerialized, the construction loses solidity. Rem Koolhaas affirms: architecture is like a lead ball shackled to a convict's foot. The latter can do nothing except rid himself of it, corroding it and hollowing it out with the help of a teaspoon. Matter and chiaroscuro are replaced by transparency and light.

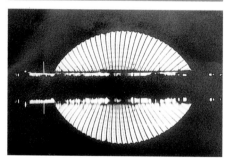

This page: Toyo Ito, Cupola O (Odate, Japan, 1997). Opposite page: Jean Nouvel, Cartier Foundation (Paris, 1991-94).

The language of information science is also rigorously based on a relational basis. Derrick de Kerckhove observes:

> It does not matter what values you attribute to the symbols of a computer language, as if the program follows the rigid rules of its logic, it will work. This is the fundamental paradox of the alphabet and the computer. They are both completely independent of the meanings attributed to them and at the same time they only exist to reproduce and manipulate sequences of values and meanings.

In other words, the computer is a machine that can make enormously complicated transformations extremely rapidly. To understand this, we can apply the same method of enquiry to the computer as was used to examine the *3 stoppages étalon*. We can distinguish four transformations.

The first is *translation*. Information is translated from one language into another: from the language used as a user interface, to the programming language, to the machine language, as far as the open/closed code that enables the flow of electrons.

The second transformation is *atomization*. Objects are dissected and fragmented until their materiality dissolves, to the point that they become pure energy and movement. Atomization enables their complexity to be reduced to a few basic elements, facilitating the matching game and making it possible to structure projections from one language to another, from one medium to another.

The third transformation is *logicization*. Arguments are reduced to pre-defined standard logic. The rules are so generalized and abstract that, at the level of machine language, all the relations between the phrases can be translated into basic logical formulas (that, in the last resort, form part of truth tables). As a result, every application can be used indifferently for apparently antithetical purposes (using a data base program, for example, it is possible to file books, manage customers, organize the shopping, estimate apartments).

The fourth transformation is *metaphorization*. The computer requires a constant effort to be made in terms of formal transpositions. In this way, we see a series of relations through another series, enabling us to store and amplify experiences that would otherwise elude us because we would be unable to express them adequately. This establishes relations not only between contents (sounds that are transformed into images, for example), but also man and machine: a prime example is the use of the metaphor of the desk or window in the structure of the computer interface or the organization of hypertexts.

3.2 Metamorphosis

Owing to these four transformations (translation, atomization, logicization, metaphorization), objects are reduced to pure formal relations. They lose their materiality and become information. Deprived of weight, information can travel inside electric fields; it can be exchanged, processed and stored.

We can dictate words to a computer, translate them into writing, reconvert them into impulses, send them by telephone and transform them into music or a drawing. In other words, we can trigger off an almost infinite series of mutations through a constant play of projections: whether these are translations, permutations, anamorphoses or even metaphors.

Seen from this historical perspective, in which language can only be regenerated on the condition that it becomes volatile, Wittgenstein, the architect, and Duchamp, the artist, were undoubtedly two sensors, two antennae that captured an epoch-making upheaval.

On the other hand, Wittgenstein, the figure who inspired the Vienna Circle and logical neopositivism, was the inventor of the truth tables and modern symbolic logic. And Duchamp was profoundly influenced by the discoveries in mathematics, geometry and physics made in the early 20th century. We need only remember his assiduous association with Poincaré's thought and his syntactic-relational approach to knowledge: "What can be affirmed by science – affirmed the French scientist, the founder of non-Euclidean geometry – are not objects themselves [...], but only relations between them. Outside these relations, there is no knowable reality."

Eisenman and Kosuth, with their obsessions for linguistics, structuralism, Chomsky's generative grammar and formal logic, resume, update and expand the experimentation of a language that has entered a new age, that of information technology.

12. A NEW ECOLOGY

Electronics compels us to stop thinking of construction as an abstract art and, in particular, of walls as part of a formal composition based on geometric rules. The wall, Wines affirms, must become "a filter that receives and transmits a wealth of information [...] just like a television" and space must become a medium which you pass through, picking up the information with which it is organized. The challenge is therefore to transform nature into architecture and, vice versa, conceive architecture as a natural element structured by communication flows.

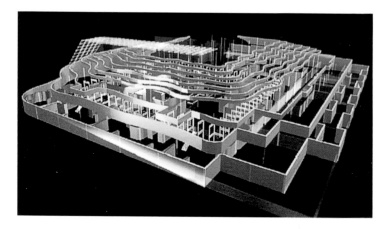

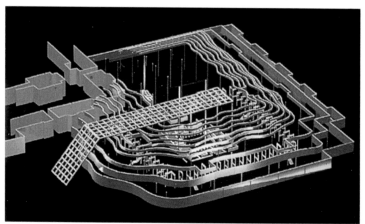

Opposite page: James Wines and the SITE Group, National Museum (Riyadh, Saudia Arabia, 1997): design schemes. This page, top: James Wines and the SITE Group, Aquatorium (Chattanooga, Tennessee, 1997): model; bottom, location plan.

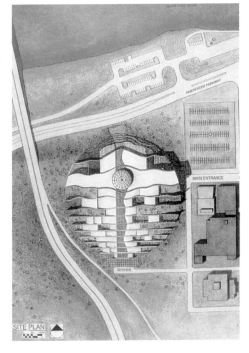

To sum up: the means used by the computer is projection, and its purpose is mutation.

Marshall McLuhan also had the same intuition, although he approached it from a different direction. As early as 1964, he affirmed that the computer would produce changes in the proportion, rhythm or schemes of human relations. In other words, it could change the way in which we think, in which we articulate language, in which we live. A well-known precedent was the invention of alphabetical writing: this not only led to the production of books, but obliged us to structure thought by organizing it into words, phrases, chapters; it broke down the barriers of local reality by encouraging the exchange of information; it facilitated the onset of individualism and free will; it established the predominance of sight over the other senses and lessened the role of hearing and the spoken word; it fostered the birth of the scientific spirit and experimental observation.

With the advent of electronics, McLuhan affirms, all man's extensions, including cities, will be translated into information systems. Thus, in the same way as the industrial society was transformed into a gigantic machine, the information society will resemble a complex nervous system, ready to capture data from the outside and transmit them for reprocessing. This reprocessing will imply a continuous metamorphosis. To the point that we lose sight of the original information, or doubt that it ever existed.

3.3 Dematerialized architecture

Let us return to architecture and to 1996, the year that Kenneth Frampton's book, *Studies in Tectonic Culture*, was published. In his last chapter, Frampton warns his reader: in contemporary architecture, form is dematerialized, the construction is losing solidity. He gives a few figures: in new buildings, the cost of the structure has fallen from 80% to 20%. Mobile partitions have increased from 3% to 20%. Only 12.5% is now spent on the facade. But, above all, installations now account for 35%. This means that, in a new building, the shell is becoming increasingly secondary, whereas growing importance is attributed to performance, monitoring systems, bioclimatic controls, technical devices.

To use McLuhan's metaphor: in building, the nervous system is dominating the skeleton and muscle structure.

The objects of Frampton's aversion are the new architectural experiments and deconstructivism. To his way of thinking, these have pushed the aesthetics of transparency beyond all limits, reducing facades to mere screens, having swallowed technology, cybernetics, multimedia. This calls for a new rigour, a syntax of construction (namely tectonics), a return to the materiality of the object. And also the need to rediscover the language of Semper, the mid-American Wright, Perret, Mies, Kahn, Utzon and Scarpa, to each of whom he dedicates a chapter. He never even mentions the work of Libeskind, Koolhaas, Hadid, Gehry or Eisenman, although he does dedicate the final chapter to Renzo Piano, who continues to work with the new technologies – now far from the excesses of the Pompidou Centre – returning them to a classical form.

Frampton's silence regarding the protagonists of contemporary architecture and, in particular, Eisenman is emblematic, on historic grounds if none other. It was Frampton who launched the group of Five Architects (Eisenman, Graves, Hejduk, Gwathmey, Meier) in 1969 at a meeting organized at the Museum of Modern Art by the Conference of Architects for the Study of Environment, and three years later he contributed a challenging critical essay to the volume *Five Architects*. Moreover, Frampton had worked with Eisenman at the Institute for Architecture and Urban Studies, as well as on the magazine *Oppositions*. From this reason Frampton might have been expected to show an interest in Eisenman's latest works after the latter had resumed professional practice in 1982 and developed his earlier projective work on cardboard houses, orientating it towards mutation, namely, the computer-inspired transformation of elementary geometric shapes into non-conventional shapes, often taken from the non-linear sciences, with works like the Guardiola House in Cadiz and the Architecture Faculty at the University of Cincinnati.

3.4 The Architecture of the Jumping Universe

Having been ignored by Frampton, Eisenman is praised in the book by the multifaceted, inexhaustible (but sometimes superficial) precursor, Charles Jencks: *The Architecture of the Jumping Universe*. In this work the English critic abjures post-modern architecture, which he had helped launch, in favor of a new architecture in which, thanks to the progress of information technology, science and nature can work together to overcome the rigid and cold mechanism on which the International Style was based.

What were the foundations for this ecological-cybernetic approach? Jencks finds them in Ilya Prigogine's philosophy of nature and the Santa Fe school, but also in Thom's catastrophe theory. According to these models, the universe is a complex system that evolves in jumps (hence the book's title: *The Architecture of the Jumping Universe*), the last of which has led to the present situation, characterized by overwhelming danger – for example, the imminent ecological and demographic catastrophe – but also enormous opportunities. Thanks to electronics, the objects of our age have been humanized and, at the same time, men have been transformed into objects, in a process that is certainly positive. The intelligence of a computer that can beat Kasparov at chess does not detract from, but rather enhances the latter's skills, in the same way that a false electronic eye does not turn the wearer into an alien.

The sophistication of these machines, in which technology and nature are blended, is still countered, in the English critic's opinion, by the coarseness of an architecture based on formative concepts of a pseudorationalist age, that refuses to take into account the fact that the new technology has developed because, having reached a post-modernist stage, science has overcome the four myths of determinism, mechanicism reductionism and materialism; namely, it has started to see the world as a system in possession of life and a self-regulating capacity, like an organism that improves its equilibrium by continuous jumps in status.

This explains the image of the butterfly, opposed to that of the trap. The trap, which symbolizes the mechanical conception of the universe, *Existenzminimum* architecture, the machine for living, is only set off when, provoked by a cause, it swallows its prey and returns less than existed prior to being set off. The butterfly, which represents the universe in its organic movement, is the product of a series of creative outbursts: an organism that develops from a caterpillar to a chrysalis to a flying insect.

How can architecture make this process visible? By acquiring a spiritual dimension and borrowing the forms of its development process from nature. This explains Jencks' interest in organic forms, fractals, curving structures that move like the waves of an atom, and in everything that represents man's spiritual movement. But above all, his interest in the computer, which makes it possible for man to play an active role in this process of continuous transformation, guiding and directing it.

For Jencks, Eisenman's latest architectural works are the perfect reflection of this *cosmogenic* ideal of a highly technologicized nature, always on the boundary between natural and artificial. In short, the second Eisenman deserves greater attention than the first Eisenman, with his cardboard houses.

This attention was returned by Eisenman himself who, on the back cover of *The Architecture of the Jumping Universe*, writes: "Charles Jencks has the uncanny capacity to announce a new movement in architecture before it has begun. With Post-Modernism, he was looking to the past. Now, for the first time, with his new book on morphogenesis he is taking a look at the future."

3.5 Architecture in the age of ecology

Jenck's theses raise uncertainties, above all owing to the conviction with which the critic links ecology and cybernetics.

In the same way, Eisenman's experiments are partial and certainly do not exhaust the complexity of the problem of architectural writing in the computer age.

However, both Jencks and Eisenman appear to grasp three key aspects that elude Frampton.

First: in the same way that we have seen the birth of a civilization based on information technology, utterly different to the previous mechanical civilisation, a new architecture has also evolved that is profoundly influenced by electronic writing, an architecture with more nerves than body, to use McLuhan's imagery. Second: the new architecture has established relations with nature that are no longer characterized by diversity, but integration. This can be seen in the work of Toyo Ito: if the new Tarzan works in the media forest, there is no more antagonism or confrontation or mimesis between a static reality (architecture) and a dynamic one (nature), but both live in the general process of mutations triggered by the new computer society. Third: some protagonists have already captured the *spirit of the time* and are producing a new season of masterpieces. The architecture of our contemporary age has already started and we have not yet realized it.

James Wines, the brain of SITE Environmental Design, has been working for years on a book now being published on the relations between architecture-ecology and computer technology. Inevitably, he is compared with Jencks. In an interview, Wines affirms: "We could agree on the presuppositions" put forward by Jencks, namely, that we live in an universe where nature and technology interact, but new ideas "are always interpreted [by Jencks] according to the precepts of traditional architecture."

Hence the danger of lapsing into a superficial ecologism, namely consisting of substantially traditional architecture covered with organic forms or ecological materials.

On the contrary, the new electronic age compels us to stop thinking of construction as an abstract art and, in particular, of walls as part of a formal composition based on geometric rules. The wall must become "a filter that receives and transmits a wealth of information [...] just like a television" and space must become a medium which you pass through picking up the information with which it is organized.

Wines concludes: "Architecture merely becomes a condition: everything disappears, everything passes through and you are not involved by the form so much as by the idea." The phrase is reminiscent of Wittgenstein's observation regarding his sister's house, but whereas for the Austrian philosopher transparency was the condition through which you could glimpse the logical structure of the world, for Wines the transparency of matter enables us to grasp the link between nature and architecture: information.

The discovery of this linking factor enables us to reinterpret construction and landscape together; interior and exterior become the same thing because both form part of a single information structure: for the next century our interlocutor will be "the earth, the terrestrial globe, the most modern machine."

Wines' comments are enlightening. But probably difficult to put into practice. They call for an approach to architectonic design that is oriented towards the formalization and management of information, different from that taught in schools of architecture which tend to focus on composition and the organization of volumes according to formal, geometric, rhythmic, proportional or even discordant principles.

3.6 A new architecture

To a certain extent, however, things themselves help us to change our attitude to architecture. It is building that is becoming more computerized, prompted once again by the overpowering force of the engineers.

Let us go back to Frampton's findings: installations now account for over a third of the cost of the entire building. In the future, this figure will change, rising even higher. This can be explained by two factors: the development of the so-called intelligent systems and the introduction of new sustainable technologies which will gradually integrate or replace those used now, which will be proved inadequate in ecological terms. There is an enormous difference between these systems and traditional methods. Just think, for example, of the massive nineteenth-century walls and a technologically innovative wall.

By its inertia, the masonry mass must submit to changes in the external environmental situation. It is characterised by heaviness, opacity, permanence. In contrast, an innovative wall can activate sensors and thereby react to changes in the external situation by producing mutations. It is light, flexible and fragile. 52-53

The masonry mass acts like a barrier to information: it blocks out everything that tries to pass through it. On the other hand, the sensitive wall resembles a transmitter: it communicates in order to activate appropriate strategies.

Let's now consider a traditional building and a technologically advanced one. The equilibrium of the first consists in interacting as little as possible with the environment. The second – to return to McLuhan's image used by Toyo Ito – lives through contact with the outside, it acts like skin, like a nervous sys-

13. A MEMBRANE-LIKE BUILDING

The equilibrium of the traditional building consists in interacting as little as possible with the environment. The technologically advanced building lives through contact with the outside, it acts like skin, like a nervous system, like a membrane.

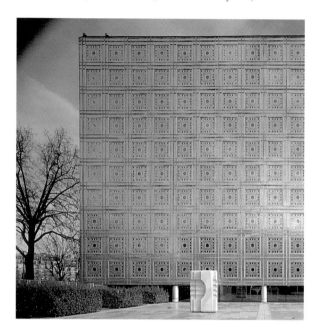

Opposite page: Jean Nouvel, Institute of the Arab World (Paris, 1981-87). Top: detail of the facade; bottom left: the light-sensitive darkening mechanism on the windows; right: inside the library. This page: Tokyo, images of the city.

tem. Like a membrane, if we do not want to push the parallel with human physiology too far.

Let us try to draw a historical parallel. In the late nineteenth century, engineers introduced reinforced concrete into construction, compelling the reluctant architects to change their formal vocabulary, making them realize that we live in an industrial society that could be clearly recognized in the thin skeletal frame of the pilotis.

At the start of the new millennium, it will again probably be the engineers who will introduce change and information through the intelligent and ecological building, obliging architects to give them form. At the moment, there may be no more Wrights, Mies or Le Corbusiers, but the Perrets, Eiffels and Behrens of the new age certainly exist already.

We cite only a possible parallel (maybe enlightening, or maybe misleading) between Perret's work in Rue Franklin **64** and Nouvel's designs for the Arab World Institute.

A wall, fully sensitive to the light but overburdened by formal references already over-used by the Arab culture, recalls the concrete walls of Rue Franklin, not completely freed from the network of nineteenth-century classicism.

3.7 A new language

A new way of expressing language is being born, independent of any explicit conceptual, formal or technical reflection on electronics. Primarily because the introduction of computers and drawing programmes probably represents the most outstandingly innovative element in the organization and structure of architectural studies. And every new technology, even if used in the most traditional and least uncertain way, leads to the discovery of new features.

In order to understand which, it may be interesting to examine an essay by Sergio Lepri on word processing. According to Lepri, three innovations are introduced by this technique:

– oral elements are introduced into the drafting of the text: you think as you write using the computer; the text can be corrected as many times as you want, without having to worry about making mistakes, changing idea, carelessness;

– the language is more alive, more simple, less difficult,

parataxis predominates over hypotaxis, i.e., there are more coordinated propositions than subordinate ones; the sentence is broken up and becomes shorter;

– there are more rhetorical figures of the metaphor-simile-oxymoron type, and therefore a greater level of creativeness and semantic variety.

Lepri concludes: using word-processing we have "rejected sophisticated and learned forms of speech in favour of simpler language which is easier to understand, closer to people; in many cases, however, especially where the composition is performed in haste, stereotypes and idioms are used which, although reducing the quality of the text, do not detract from its intelligibility." The new aspects introduced by word-processing can also be found in CAD drawings:

– *simplification of the language and inclusion of oral elements*: this is made possible by verifying functional standards using simple applicative routines; the machine is set up for basic, simple, effective, precise writing, far removed from the incredible delicacy of traditional drawing; the greater possibility of control and multimedia reproduction of the surrounding reality, in particular, the urban landscape, even when degraded and peripheral;

– *prevalence of parataxis over hypotaxis*: this derives from the greater simplicity of working by matching and the possibility of clarifying and bringing out hierarchies that would otherwise be obscure and complex; the preparation of ready-made libraries of objects; the additive logic of formal and functional layers;

– *the predilection for rhetorical figures*: this is stimulated by the simplicity of organizing metaphors and anamorphoses, above all of an organic nature, using simple transformation commands; the possibility of introducing external sounds, images and colours and working on them; the possibility of realising complex 3D forms that are difficult to control using traditional drawing instruments.

The parallels with word-processing also include the limitations: the indiscriminate use of libraries and ready-made elements coupled with the ease of making duplications makes many CAD drawings anonymous, flat and repetitive.

14. The house as an interior telescope

To Jung, the house at Bollingen not only becomes a space in which he can be alone with himself, it represents the concrete expression of the unconscious, conceived as a bridge linking man, through archetypes and myths, with death and the eternal world of the past. The house as a purely transparent concept was therefore countered by the house as a purely interior concept, like an interior telescope.

The tower at Bollingen in 1923, 1927, 1935 and 1955.

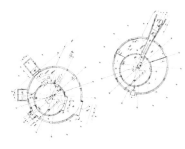

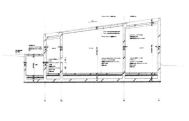

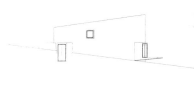

Kazuyo Seyma, House in the Wood *(Chino, Japan, 1992-94). Left, from top to bottom: the central space illuminated from the top, access to the central space, the service areas along the ring area. Right, from top to bottom: plans, north elevation and cross-section.*

4. Simulation

4.1 The art of memory

To recapitulate: the instrument used by computers is projection, its purpose is mutation. But its product is simulation. This is the last word in the triad to be examined.

But first we must go back in time. Simulation did not originate with computer science. In the book *The Art of Memory*, Frances A. Yates tells us that a very effective way of remembering complex events was used in ancient times: the trick was to imagine a house with many rooms and to locate a key phrase in each room. By mentally passing through every room (one phrase was in the hall, another in the living room, another in the dining room), the entire event, which might otherwise have been forgotten, could be easily reconstructed.

They also used another expedient: in order to remember each phrase precisely, they turned it into a person whose image represented the phrase. For example, according to Cicero, the image of an old man lying on a bed in a room, with a cup of poison beside him, a writing-tablet on the left and holding a goat's testicles in his hand represented a man killed by poison, with the hope of an inheritance in a crime with several witnesses and accomplices. Seneca the Elder, a master of rhetoric, could repeat two thousand names in the same order that they had been spoken by assigning each to a room.

By giving the event physical status, the Romans could relive their memories in every form: even backwards. Instead of going from the dining room to the bedrooms, all they had to do was invert the order. Moreover, just like a chest of drawers, they could open a drawer (namely a room) with their imagination and see the contents. The practical results of the method were prodigious and they acquired added importance because of the rarity of using written forms of memorization owing to the high cost of parchment. In a class of over two hundred students, each of whom recited a verse, Seneca could repeat them all in reverse order, starting with the last and working backwards right to the beginning.

From time immemorial there has been a close relationship between the virtuality of the mind and the reality of facts, between the way in which we organize thought and architectonic forms. And vice versa. As was seen earlier, Wittgenstein tried to translate his own philosophy into buildings. Expressions like "focus one's thoughts," "reflect," "give structure to one's thoughts," all refer to space and construction.

Gaston Bachelard, a critic and epistemologist, has written numerous works on space as a mental structure. The psychoanalyst Jung also attempted to petrify his own unconscious mind as a form of construction.

4.2 Jung's interior telescope

The history of this building is told in the book by C.G. Jung, entitled *Memories, Dreams, Reflections*. In 1922 Jung bought a 68 plot of land in Bollingen, near Zürich, on which to build a house overlooking the lake. He first intended to construct a circular hut, almost like a primitive dwelling with a hearth in the center and bunks round the walls. Then, he decided to build a two-story circular house, a tower. "To me it represented the maternal hearth. But I soon realized that I had not fully expressed everything I wanted to say." After four years, he added on an extension. Four years later, still unsatisfied, he transformed the extension into another tower with a room in which he could live alone. He decorated it with paintings to illustrate his wanderings "from the world to solitude, from the present to eternity."

In 1935, he added a courtyard with a loggia thereby satisfying his desire for a small enclosed area: "I needed a wider space, open to the sky and to nature." The addition of this last part created a set of four: a symbolic element that represented the perfection of three (trinity) at the moment of its humanization (four). Of the four elements, the part that represented his ego was the central building squeezed between the two towers, symbolizing the tension of opposing forces. In 1955, he added another floor to the architectural counterpart of his ego. "I could not have done so earlier; I would have regarded it as a presumptuous and emphatic affirmation of myself; instead, now it represents the superiority of conscience attained in old age."

This external symbolism corresponds to a more profound level. The building was first started in 1923, the year his mother died, and completed in 1955, a year before his wife's death.

15. The labyrinth

Hypothesis no. 1: if architectural forms change, our brains will be prompted to think differently, to be structured using more flexible, less oppressive forms, to explore new dimensions of thought. Culminating in an ability to overturn our destinies, seeing life not as a temporal linear sequence with a beginning and an end, as suggested by the linear and homogeneous space-time of our constructed environment. Hypothesis no. 2: the labyrinth is the dimension of our contemporaneousness: terrible but stimulating.

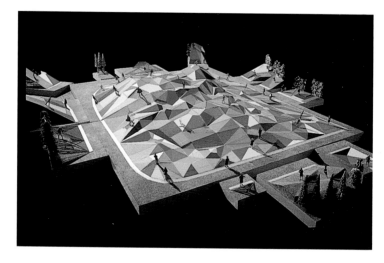

Arakawa and Madeline Gins, Sites of Reversible Destiny *(published photos, 1994).*

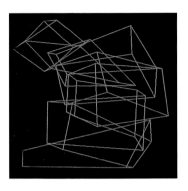

Daniel Libeskind, extension to the Victoria & Albert Museum (London, 1996, project under construction): top left, conceptual diagram; top right, perspective section. Bottom: model.

"These two dates," states Jung, "convey a meaning, because the Tower is linked to the dead." While excavating, they found the corpse of a drowned French soldier and this convinces Jung even more that his theory is correct. Like the huts used by many primitive people, the tower is positioned in relation to the earth through the body of a dead man: the construction therefore symbolically links the underworld to the heavens. The tower therefore not only becomes a space in which Jung can be alone with himself, it represents the concrete expression of the unconscious, conceived, precisely like the building he has erected, as a bridge linking man, through archetypes and myths, with death and the eternal world of the past. I am, he adds, "the age-old son of the mother": of the mother, the earth, who is the unconscious.

Jung's approach is reflected in the work of many earlier and contemporary philosophers. Among his precursors is Goethe, who retraces the ritual foundations of the home in the intense episode of *Elective Affinities*. Among his contemporaries is Heidegger, whose conception of the home is highly symbolic. Jung designed a machine against time to counter the process of becoming. Using the words of Horace, he later described the tower as *aere perennis*, lasting longer than bronze. Not only because it was built in solid stone, but because the three spatial dimensions annul the past and future, turning them into a sort of eternal present.

4.3 A city where no one dies

Let us come back to 1997. There is an exhibition of Arakawa at the Guggenheim Museum in Soho.

Arakawa is a Japanese artist who moved to New York in 1961. With a conceptual formation, like Kosuth, Atkinson, Baldwin, he is interested in the relations between language and the tangible world. For Arakawa, language is the space of representation and is therefore structured like architecture. And vice versa: architecture expresses the structure of our language. There is a close formal analogy between the way in which the scientific conceptions of the Western world are organized and the structure of our cities: classification, distinction, order, hierarchy. This gives rise to a hypothesis: if architectural forms change, our brains will be prompted to think differently, to be structured using more flexible, less oppressive forms, to explore new dimensions of thought. Culminating in an ability to overturn our destinies, seeing life not as a temporal linear sequence with a beginning and an end, as suggested by the linear and homogeneous space-time of our constructed environment.

Our aim, Arakawa suggests, is to "to learn how not to die," and the only way of achieving this is to overcome our mental structure, which now projects us towards the idea of finitude.

Arakawa, in collaboration with Gins, then dedicated himself to architectonic design, with the aid of computers. He produces projects in which our conception of space is radically overturned: labyrinths in which we are lost, anamorphic structures that deform the Euclidean space to which we are accustomed, spaces in which to dissolve the corporal dimension, curved surfaces that deny our spatial categories based on opposites like inside-outside, above-below, right-left.

Breaking down meaning, creating new chains of events, neutralizing subjectivity: these are just some of the aims of these new projects, a few of which are realized in Japan: *Ubiquitous Site *Nagi's Ryoanji* Architectural Body* at the Museum of Contemporary Art in Nagi and *Site of Reversible Destiny* at [72] Yoro. The exhibition of Arakawa's works attracts a reasonable number of visitors, like his architectural projects in Japan which are visited by followers and those who are curious to find out more. The public are attracted not so much by the Nietzschean perspective of overcoming death, through the introduction and elaboration of a new concept of time and space (there are numerous affinities between Arakawa's *reversible destiny* and Nietzsche's *eternal return*), but by the curiosity of trying out these architectural forms, which differ so radically from those to which we are accustomed.

But also by the surprise of seeing spaces and cities created using the computer that, behind their apparent extraneousness, point to new directions for research.

4.4 The labyrinth

For the moment let us leave Arakawa, whose goals certainly seem utopian to us Europeans, materialists and without hope.

16. THE INFORMATION TECHNOLOGY REVOLUTION

Walter Gropius, Bauhaus (Dessau, Germany, 1926).

Circuit diagram of a chip made by Texas Instruments, 1985.

And let us come back to a semiologist who undoubtedly forms part of our scientific culture: Umberto Eco.

In an recent meeting on the subject of the third millennium, Umberto Eco reiterated his idea of history: less Eurocentric, more open to the understanding of non-Western civilisations. In addition, he proposed setting up a museum in the form of a labyrinth, consisting of paths, each of which is dedicated to a special story. For example, in this museum, the history of Europe would run parallel to the history of America until 1492, when the two paths lead into a single room, from which point they move forward together. The user can chose his or her own path. With the possibility (ensured perhaps by the see-through walls) of watching parallel historical paths.

Umberto Eco has always been attentive to architecture: his early essays (*The Open Work* and *La struttura assente*) are important for the construction of a modern interpretation of architectonic language. His novels always include an accurate description of buildings and spaces, even verging on pedantry. One need only think of the abbey described in *The Name of the Rose* and the library it contained.

Eco's ability to make conceptual structures real in architectural terms reminds us of Cicero and the art of memory: each event corresponds to a space and the events are linked together by paths. With the sole and by no means secondary difference that while Cicero's conceptual structure refers to a traditional house made up of rooms connected by a corridor, Umberto Eco's museum resembles a labyrinth or perhaps a hypertext, namely an electronic book in which the linear structure of the printed page has been totally overturned. As George P. Landow suggests, "the reader can choose from a number of different itineraries to follow, think or read in a non-sequential manner".

4.5 Virtual

Wittgenstein, Eco, Arakawa, Cicero and Jung all show that the mind uses spatial metaphors to visualize its own conceptual structures. And that the virtual space of the mind is enriched by continuous comparison with the real architectural use of space. Let us go back to computer technology.

William J. Mitchell notes: electronic spaces apparently deny any form of geometry. They are logical, mental spaces. Take the Internet, for example: "The Net is fundamentally and profoundly *antispatial*. It has nothing to do with Piazza Navona or Copley Square. You never know where it is and you cannot describe its forms or proportions, or tell a tourist how to get there. The Net is an environment – located nowhere in particular, but at the same time everywhere. You do not go there, but you can gain access using a command (*log in*) from wherever you are. By doing so, you do not visit it in the traditional sense; you are only uttering a word which will guarantee your entry, in the same way that you might say: *Open sesame.*" Yet the net uses spatial metaphors: you have an address, you search for a site, you navigate in cyberspace.

Without using these metaphors you would get lost: the overwhelming success of Macintosh – which forced IBM to abandon the more abstract Dos for the more spatial Windows – can be summed up as the user-friendly use of an interface which is the perfect metaphor of a desk.

There are a surprising number of affinities between this electronic desk and the strategies adopted by Cicero and Seneca. It is made up of folders, each of which contains other folders, in precisely the same way as the rooms of memory contrived by our ancestors to organise their own memories.

Seen from this point of view, the term virtual is none other than the formalization of thought, the transformation of thought into architectonic space. Spatialization can be very simple. The folders used by Macintosh are particularly simple and are therefore immediately perceptible by all since they use systems of spatial formalization that have been consolidated for thousands of years. Arakawa's formalizations, on the other hand, follow new forms of thought and therefore generate consternation and discomfiture.

4.6 Where we are going

Let us go back to our initial definition.

The dictionary gives the following definition for the term project: "1. Jut out or protrude, cast; 2. Cause to fall on a screen." Projection implies a throwing forward, projecting in order to place the concept outside ourselves where it can be elaborated.

Because of our idealist mentality, we tend to underestimate this process and focus all our attention on the end result: the fully formed thought. We are often led to consider the means on which we have projected thought as being irrelevant: if we have written it on a sheet of paper, if we have input it using a keyboard, if we have created it using a 3D model or mathematical formula.

The means, as linguistic experts never tire of repeating, are a key aspect. Not only because without them we could not perform complex logical operations. For example, try solving the multiplication 3,489,765 x 3465 without using a piece of paper. Or formulating a very long argument without fixing the points somehow or somewhere (this explains why, without being able to use paper, Cicero and Seneca used the metaphor of the house, namely another medium, that of spatialization).

But above all, because every medium – paper, drawings, computers – imposes its own laws in the long run. By using one instrument instead of another, thought sounds out its own possibilities, but is always guided in one direction, along the itineraries used by that particular medium. What are the paths used by the computer? We will only know when we have tried them out. However, we can already formulate a hypothesis: research imposed on architecture by electronic language concerns mutation; we have seen this through the very different works of Koolhaas, Ito, Eisenman, Libeskind, Hadid and Arakawa.

In the future, the computer will allow and guarantee new experiences in the field of virtualization, which – as we have seen – is the destiny of mutation. If architecture wishes to play an important role in this process, as it is trying to do, it may become the spatialization and concretization for the development of thought. This will open up new horizons for language.

And it does not matter if much of the old architectural language which we have grown accustomed to disappears or alters its meaning to the point that it seems remote. After all, the linguist John Austin is right when he asserts that words alone do not mean anything. It is the contents, the life and the thought they convey that are meaningful.

Hyper-Architecture
Afterword by Antonino Saggio

1.1 Fluidity Squared

Let us again reconsider several lines of thought. "Fluidity" is the key word in information technology. The single unit of information is not set on a support (stone, parchment, papyrus, canvas, paper) but is made up of an electric impulse. It changes at the speed of light, but it is above all the relationship connecting it to other atoms which changes instantaneously. The world of information technology is, in fact, like a mobile web, in which the fundamental elements are the interconnections. If this fluidity describes it, then it is the dynamic quality which characterizes this world. We can regroup units, one with the other, put them into a hierarchy of innumerable relationships and create models. And, with the variations of an atom, verify change in the entire system or, changing the sense, the order or interfacing of the connections, forming different worlds.

Let's take the simplest of examples. Even if we are often not aware of it, we write differently on the computer. The brain moves faster, we can always improve and change the words, imagine more and create more metaphors, but how many clearly understand that it is precisely the interconnection which is the key? As always, it is artists who understand first. An avant-garde novelist, for example, writes by putting down a spontaneous and chaotic flow of events, stories and characters. He abandons himself like a torrent. On a mountain of data, he then records information (that is he adds a series of key words, "man, nature, Claudia" to the facts) and, by way of computer-guided research, builds associations, structures and narrative forms.

Thus various stories are born, from which the most significant can now be chosen. His universe is malleable.

Now, it is clear that if we are dealing with architectural spatiality, where we must use a type of architectural "writing" to understand the meaning of the information technology revolution, the answer cannot reside only in the primary level, the atoms and their capacity for change, but must go deeper, right into their dynamic interconnection. It is this relationship, this pattern, as defined by Fritjof Capra, that is the real engine of this era, including architecture. But how?

1.2 Metaphorization

Project, mutate, simulate; these are words run through by a subject which once again should be reflected upon: that of rhetorical figures of speech (oxymoron, metonymy and many others still, but let us stop, for simplicity, at metaphor). Rhetorical figures of speech, which develop – powerfully, specifically– when writing on the computer, basically create actual interconnections, a method of relating various data in order to send messages and convince. The rhetorical figure of speech has a potentially dynamic aspect which other relations (cause-effect, first-last, above-below) do not have. If one says, "You are beautiful like the moon," the message is multi-directional: there is a key to reading it but others are possible (with variations in culture, moments, countries, etc.).

The messages of our electronic age are ever more metaphorical and ever less assertive. It is the enormous mass of information which imposes links, though freer, more open links. An example? Advertising in the industrial world used to be assertive. This soap washes whiter; these jeans are more resistant. We know that advertising today sends out messages which are all figurative, all metaphorical. It induces, substantially through the use of rhetorical figures of speech, an association between a series of elements and the product; frequently without even showing the product and often without even describing it. The narration is bought first, the living utopia that the product promises, then its form, and it is absolutely taken for granted that this works. The container wins completely over the content.

But this process of metaphorization, induced by a sense which goes beyond industrial mechanisms to open up a freer and more multi-directional sphere of messages, this process based on the dynamic interconnections of the metaphor, permeates everything in our era. It is sufficient to look at design and the sphere of architecture, itself more resistant to change.

A building is no longer good only if it works, is solid, spatially rich, livable, etc., but also because it recalls something other than itself. Libeskind traces a dramatic "Z" to tell the drama of the Holocaust; Eisenman, a dance of tellurian plates; Gehry, a lotus flower in his auditorium; Domenig, cracks and fissures which collide with one another in his house. We know that the process of metaphorization permeates a large part of the architecture of today and that its fundamental field is a new interiorization of the landscape and the relationship between man and nature. This has been learnt, or almost. In order to go further into still tough terrain, we must return to electronics and especially its center: interconnections.

1.3 To Bill

After the invention of the personal computer (we are speaking of around 1977), the first revolution in information technology occurred in 1984 with the wide-scale distribution of a revolutionary new operating system (in other words, the method utilized by the user to operate the computer). The basis was, naturally, metaphorization.

No longer were there abstruse codes which appeared on an inanimate screen, but objects on a desktop-screen. To open or duplicate a document, one highlighted it with a cursor and clicked on it; to copy it, it was dragged to another location; to change its name, one simply rewrote it on its small icon; to throw it away, it was dumped into the trash. This method of proceeding by metaphor, a metaphor taken from the real world and applied to electronics, was also incorporated into the programs. There was a large table of instruments for design; to write, a scroll similar to a typewriter; to draw, a universal drafting device. This first level of metaphorization was fundamental; since it introduced millions of people to using the computer, it was important that it become a standard on more platforms.

However, the second invention was even more important and so innovative that only today is its significance being effectively understood. It was in 1987 and a genius, William Atkinson, after having made a substantial contribution to the construction of the metaphor of the desk, developed another new idea.

17. FLOWS

Vasilij Kandinskij, Composition no. 8, *1923.*

Why not give the user not only a pre-packaged metaphor, but the possibility of creating metaphors himself? Why not work, in other words, with a metaphor "creating" tool?

So Bill created Hypercard, which is just that; a computer environment which creates metaphors. The user puts down information under any form (designs, writing, numbers, tables, animated sequences, three-dimensional objects and many others) and either at the same time, or later, performs two fundamental actions: creates the connections and organizes a metaphorical environment.

The most banal of these environments is the card, where the information is contained and where, clicking on each item, the user can proceed in the network of relations; but along with the card, there can be millions of other metaphorical environments. The production of an artist is in his virtual studio, a virtual lesson is held on a blackboard, shopping is done at home in a real store, but more importantly the user can dream and build worlds which do not exist. In brief, this is what is called *Hypertext*. The basis is the interconnection between the units of information and the creation of a metaphorical environment in which these interconnections are located. The end result is that the user has methods which are non-compulsory, non-sequential. He can follow courses already preset or find his own new one. In some way, it is as if the novelist mentioned earlier gave the data his structure of meaning and at the same time left the possibility open for the reader to create his own.

By now, this system is everywhere, since, while in 1987 it was only relegated to the single computer, Internet today is a planetary web which connects many worlds of information to each other.

1.4 Hypertext Painter

Let us return to architecture and ask ourselves: can we also work in architecture on this second level? Can we work on an architecture which is not only metaphorical, but also a "creator of metaphors," which leaves its own decodification open, free, structured/non-structured and suggests and offers to the user the possibility of constructing "his own story?"

To put it briefly, the true end is not only the metaphorization of the first level, but that of the second. To manage not only to imagine an architecture which is fluid, metaphorical and open, which plays on the skin like new, immaterial sensors, which completely assimilates and values a multimediality which moves into systems of control and information, but which is above all capable of generating other metaphors and causing others to be generated, those of life and its advancement into this new dimension: the entire past and the entire future.

Can we work on this ambitious and very difficult concept as the frontier of our task? Finally, does a more adequate word exist than Hyper-Architecture to describe this challenge?

What can help us? Can it really be that this sense, this need, in a century so rich in events, personalities and geniuses, has not already been at least guessed at?

In the architecture of this last decade, several very important discoveries have been made regarding the figurative arts.

Gehry in his last period owes quite a lot to Boccioni and his concept of trajectory, to that force of going beyond the plastic quality of the isolated object toward an atmospheric vibration. Peter Eisenman has adopted more than one technique from the vibration of Duchamp and Balla. The dripping technique of Pollock is touched upon in various types of research into new forms of landscape and the construction of nature, but who has really understood the spatiality inherent in Kandinsky?

Atoms and geometric worlds are inserted into his paintings in a liquid amoeba, but these figures interconnect with lines, superimpositions, interconnections. The overall whole emanates energy and seems like a Hypertext because it can move itself continuously; it has a structure photographed in a brief moment, but its value is not the static moment of Mondrian, but rather in the possibility of evolving, being free and open. Certainly, we know that without Impressionist orientalism and the breaking of the square box, there would be no Wright, that the space of Braque foreshadowed the Bauhaus, that the energy of movement and Expressionist deformation were related to Mendelsohn and Scharoun, that neo-plastic designs transmigrated almost directly into Rietveld and Mies. We know that artists have a spatiality which transmigrates into architecture.

But the fluid, liquid, submarine, metaphorical, symbolic and interconnected spatiality of Kandinsky (and Mirò and Klee) is, without information technology, impossible to conceptualize in architecture. With information technology, on the other hand, this becomes almost vaguely intuitable.

This is perhaps what we are attempting to do with this strange word: Hyper-Architecture.

Saggio@axrma.uniroma1.it

Further reading

The pages of this book have been influenced by two authors in particular: Paul K. Feyerabend and Marshall McLuhan. Paul Feyerabend is a philosopher of science who became fashionable in the Seventies, but was then overlooked in favor of the more soothing but less acute Karl Popper. His key work is *Against Method*, New Left Books, London 1975. An excellent introduction to Feyerabend's work can be found in his autobiography, published posthumously under the title *Killing Time*, Univ. of Chicago, 1995. The works of Marshall McLuhan, sociologist, philosopher and new media critic also received a similar reception in Italy: initial attention followed by premature oblivion. He is only remembered for a few brilliant remarks, now repeated by everyone as tired clichés: the "global village" or "the medium is the message." Three factors contribute to the scarce attention received by McLuhan's work: the daring interdisciplinary links, the language which is both obscure and terroristically metaphoric, and lastly the unpalatable nature of his approach to the masters of Italian culture. For an initial overview of McLuhan's work it may be useful to start with *Understanding Media: The Extensions of Man* (McGraw-Hill, New York 1964). A popular but rigorous introduction to McLuhan's thought is given by Derrick de Kerckhove in *Brainframes* (Bosch & Keuning, Utrecht 1991) and *La civilisation vidéo-chretienne* (Ed. Retz, Paris 1990). A reflection on some McLuhanian themes is found in the works of the sociologist Franco Ferrarotti, whose recent *La perfezione del nulla* (Laterza, Bari 1997) is recommended, and the readily accessible work by Matteo Sanfilippo and Vincenzo Matera, *Da Omero al cyberpunk* (Castelvecchi, Roma 1995).

1. ARCHITECTURE IN THE AGE OF ELECTRONICS

1.1 An antecedent: the Pompidou Centre
It is interesting to compare Frampton's rejection of the Pompidou Centre with the unconditional enthusiasm for Renzo Piano's later work in *Tectonic Culture* (MIT Press, Boston 1995). See the discussion in § 3.3 "Dematerialised architecture." The book published in the series Universale di Architettura edited by Bruno Zevi is: Giuseppe Marinelli, *Il Centro Beaubourg a Parigi, "macchina" e segno architettonico* (Dedalo libri, Bari 1978). The text is enhanced by interesting comments by Jacobus Bakema, Edoardo Bruno, Peter Cook, Ugo la Pietra, Achille Perilli and Bruno Zevi.

1.2 Electronic Bauhaus
The terrible beauty of the twentieth century and the history of ZKM are described in the book by Rem Koolhaas and Bruce Mau, *S, M, L, XL* (010 Publishers, Rotterdam 1995) which brings together, almost in a sort of hypertext, all Koolhaas' main works and publications.

1.3 A library like a microchip
The issue of *El Croquis* dedicated to Toyo Ito is no. 71 of 1995. *El Croquis* has dedicated excellent monographs to the most interesting contemporary architects. The

most recent include: Rem Koolhaas (no. 79), Frank Gehry (nos. 74-75), Jean Nouvel (nos. 65-66), Zaha Hadid (no. 73), Peter Eisenman (no. 83), Kazuyo Seyma (no. 77), Morphosis (no. 59), Enric Miralles (no. 72).

1.4 Waves in the sea of communication

The article by Toyo Ito *Tarzans in the media forest* is published in the issue of 2G (no. 2, 1997) dedicated to him. For a detailed analysis of McLuhan's concept of tactility: Derrick de Kerkhove, *The Skin of Culture*, Somerville Press, Toronto 1995. On the same subject, but seen from the architect's point of view, it is worth reading the interviews of Nouvel, Perrault, Piano, Wines, Prix, Venturi, Suzuki, Herzog published in *Sull'involucro in architettura* by Daniela Colafranceschi (Edizioni librerie Dedalo, Bari 1996). *Architecture and Disjunction* by Bernard Tschumi (MIT Press, Boston 1996) is also recommended and discusses this in *Six Concepts*.

1.5 Mies+ Futurism

On Daniel Libeskind, it is worth reading *Radix-matrix* (Prestel, Munich 1997), edited by Libeskind himself. The book, whose graphic presentation is excellent, offers a satisfactory overview of the architect's works, as well as containing his writings, essays and an intervention, with Libeskind's reply, by the philosopher, Jacques Derrida. The relationship between Balla-Eisenmann, Gehry-Boccioni is also mentioned by Antonino Saggio, *Peter Eisenman*, Testo & Immagine, Torino 1996.

2. PROJECTION

2.1 An antecedent: Duchamp

The retrospective exhibition at Palazzo Grassi in 1993 gave definitive confirmation of Duchamp's role as the keystone of contemporary art. The author of "open works" *ante litteram*, any number of interpretations have been put forward: literal, literary, symbolic, psychological, hermetic, deconstructive. Duchamp himself encouraged this, while viewing them with detached irony. The catalogue published by Bompiani to mark the occasion of the Venice exhibition serves as a good introduction to his work and some of the most accredited exegeses. Further information on Duchamp's interest in all projective procedures is given in his own writings, collected and edited by Michel Sanouillet in *Duchamp du signe* (Flammarion, Paris 1994). In particular, see p.122 ff. for his remarks on perspective and the transformations of objects from more to fewer dimensions, for example, from 5 to 4 and then 4 to 3, and so on, until you reach a single dimension. For the reader who wonders what relationship exists between Duchamp's projective arguments and the architecture of the age of electronics, we can state in advance that the entire information society is aimed at producing mutations through projections (cfr. § 3.1 "Transformations"). Those wishing to analyze further the concept of projection and transformations between universes of different dimensions should read *Flatland. A Romance of Many Dimensions* by Edwin A. Abbott (Barnes & Noble, New York 1983). Written as a novel, *Flatland* is an essential theoretical work for analyzing relations between the mind and spatial constructions and also helps to understand a number of concepts discussed in this book (for example, the third chapter on simulation). Further discussion and interpretations of *Flatland* can be found in *The Fourth Dimension. A Guided Tour of the Higher Universes* by Rudy Rucker (Houghton Mifflin Company, Boston 1984).

2.2 Projection and conceptual art

On art which describes itself through art, the best work is *La linea analitica dell'arte moderna* by Filiberto Menna (Einaudi, Torino 1975). The combination of metaphor and projection is also put forward, albeit implicitly, by Gianfranco Bettini in *La simulazione visiva* (Bompiani, Milano 1991). For Bettini, in fact, the metaphor is a sort of model, "a reasonable approximation of a reality which is difficult to grasp with precision [...]." Together with the icon, being analogic it stands out from the scientific or digital model, above all because it is not formalized on a mathematical basis and therefore cannot be immediately expressed in a binary form.

2.3 Verdussen of Utrecht

It is worth noting, almost in parenthesis, that in his tales, Borges constructs architecture with a strong conceptual character, buildings that are perhaps even more abstract than those described by Verdussen. Borges' literary architecture was examined in an exhibition at the Pompidou Centre in 1996.

2.4 Eisenman Verdussen

The story of Eisenman's *House VI* is told by the client herself in Suzanne Frank, *Peter Eisenman's House VI: The Client's Response* (Whitney Library of Design, New York 1994). On the subject of *House VI* it is also worth noting the intervention by the philosopher Richard Rorty, for whom the house is one of the masterpieces of post-Holocaust culture, namely the conscious abandonment of all hope in the idea of the rationality of history. To complete the parallel between Duchamp and Eisenman, it is worth underlining their common interest in puns (used in the titles of many of their works) and in ambiguous situations – in particular configurations where there is no clear difference between open-closed, high-low, right-left. It is also important to mention the interest of two philosophers, Lyotard and Derrida, respectively in Duchamp and Eisenman. Lastly, we underline that the language of conceptual art has not only led to Eisenman's experimentations, creating the logical and methodological bases for his second and more fertile period oriented towards computer experiments, but also to the static reflections of the neorationalist movement, also known as *La Tendenza*. The most acute – if also the most disenchanted – supporter of this movement was Manfredo Tafuri, to whose works we refer. At this point it is interesting to note that Tafuri was the author of one of the most interesting essays on Eisenman: it appears as an introduction to the volume edited by Camillo Gubitosi and Alberto Izzo, *Five Architects NY* (Officina, Roma 1976). Again on the subject of the ambiguous and fertile role of conceptualism in architecture, it is worth remembering that in 1967 Giorgio Grassi – whose work moves in completely the opposite direction to the pioneers of contemporary architecture – published an essay entitled *La costruzione logica dell'architettura*, as part of the Marsilio series Polis, in which, based on his own reflections on Wittgenstein's *Tractatus*, he explicitly affirms that architecture must be pure intellectual construction, absolute tautological transparency. On similar or, better, complementary positions, see the essays by Francesco Amendolaggine and Massimo Cacciari, entitled *Oikos, da Loos a Wittgenstein* (Officina, Roma 1975). Lastly, it is worth recalling that Frampton, who first supported Eisenman, later reached the shores of neorationalism and tectonics, assuming a conservative attitude that was extremely suspicious of the computer revolution in architecture (cfr.on this subject § 3.3 "Dematerialised architecture").

2.5 Architecture of silence

In all of his work, but in particular in *Gusto del segreto*, written together with the Italian philosopher Maurizio Ferraris (Laterza, Bari 1997), Jacques Derrida proposes a vision of the Absolute as that which is not presented, which is never given, a view which closely resembles that proposed by Eisenman through his architecture. For a lucid criticism of the mysticism of Absence, but one that can only be shared in part owing to its realistic presuppositions, see Umberto Eco, *La struttura assente* (Bompiani, Milano 1968), and later essays by the same author in which he returns to the same subject, from a slightly different viewpoint. The most recent and complete book on Wittgenstein as an architect is by Paul Wijdeveld, *Wittgenstein Architect* (Thames and Hudson, London 1994). From a critical point of view, however, the text is unsatisfactory. Zevi's writings on the subject are still up-to-date ("Logicus filosoficus anche nella modanatura" in *Cronache di architettura*, vol. IX, no. 1024), as are those by Leitner, *The architecture of Ludwig Wittgenstein. A Documentation* (New York University Press, New York 1976). Lastly, it is interesting to note that the second Wittgenstein (namely after he overcame the *Tractatus* and oriented himself towards a less algebraiciszable analysis of language) often uses architectonic metaphors. For example, when he compares language to a city made up of quarters, each of which has its own layout.

3. MUTATION

3.1 Transformations

The theme of projection and echo is linked to the reflection on the meaning of mirrors. Umberto Eco (*nomen, omen*) has discussed this theme in *Sugli specchi e altri saggi* (Bompiani, Milano 1985) and, more recently, in *Kant and the platypus* (Harcourt Brace, New York 1999). The subject was also tackled by Tomás Maldonado in *Reale e virtuale* (Feltrinelli, Milano 1992). Both authors affirm that the mirror is a projection, almost in its pure state, of reality, a perfect iconic model that can in some way represent the reflective process of knowledge (compared to Maldonado, Eco makes more concessions to conventionalism and Popperian falsification). Compared to these theories, which are still too firmly anchored to research into the *thing itself*, the analyses made by the post-structuralists appear more convincing. The latter doubt that the play of mirrors leads to definitive knowledge or increasingly approximated knowledge of reality and they introduce the concept of *drift*, namely an infinite reflection that, through a continuous play of projections from one medium to another, presents reality – or better, what appears to be reality – from new and, to a certain extent (ontologically, not structurally) arbitrary points of view. In this respect, made harsh by an unbearably abstruse style, we recommend the essays by Derrida, such as those in *Margins of Philosophy* (Univ. of Chicago 1984) and, in particular, the final essay *Firma evento contesto*, that dates back to 1968. The clearest explanation of the Derridian problem can be found in the novels by David Lodge, in particular *Small World* (Martin Secker & Warburg Ltd, London 1984). For those who appreciate the logocentric and logorrhoic writing of the post-structuralists, the most interesting reflections on the loss of the sense of reality through the endless game of mirrors in interpretations and translations are by Jean Baudrillard. The following are particularly recommended: *Le crime parfait* (Editions Galilée, Paris 1995), *The Disappearance of Art and Politics* (St. Martin Press, New York 1992) and *The ecstasy of communications* (Autonomedia, Brooklyn, N.Y. 1988). From Baudrillard it is possible to work back towards the deadly eroticizing vision of the neo-Nietzschean Bataille, and towards the more disenchanted science of Patafisica and his amusing and stimulating paradoxes.

3.2 Metamorphosis

In *Reale e virtuale* cit., Maldonado defines three categories of mutations: homological (maintaining the structure, but not the form and function), analogic (retaining the structure and function, but not the form) and isomorphic (only the form remains the same). All three types of mutation are present in the transformation processes carried out using the computer and described in this section.

3.3 Dematerialized architecture

On immateriality readers should refer to the writings of the French philosopher Jean-François Lyotard, who curated a major exhibition at the Pompidou Centre on this subject. In the architectural field the theme of immateriality marks the watershed between two different groups: the Immaterials and Tectonics. The Immaterials back Mies' language of the virtually nil (cfr. § 1.5 "Mies+Futurism") and the groups of avantgarde architects in the Seventies – including the Superstudio – who proposed great and evanescent containers or spaces deprived of architecture. The Tectonics base their activities on traditional architecture and, in particular, on Semper. Among the Immaterials, the most interesting theoretic positions are those of Toyo Ito and Rem Koolhaas (cfr. § 1.3, 1.4, 1.5). The position of Bernard Tschumi is also interesting: in *Architecture and Disjunction* cit., he proposes, against the mechanized and Taylorized architecture of *Existenzminimum* and the *Frankfurt kitchen*, a spatiality that is no longer based on the oppressive materiality of the walls, but the free movement of the bodies. As well as Frampton, the Tectonics include Vittorio Gregotti in Italy and Luis Fernández-Galiano in Spain.

3.4 The architecture of the jumping universe

The Architecture of the Jumping Universe by Charles Jencks (Academy Editions, London 1995) has a useful and up-to-date bibliography.

3.5 Architecture in the age of ecology

An essay by Wines published before the book appeared in *The Architecture of Ecology* (Academy Editions, London 1997).

3.6 A new architecture

There are increasing numbers of specialized publications dealing with the repercussions on architecture of the information technology revolution. Among the magazines, the monographic issue of *Architecture* published in June 1997, was entirely dedicated to information technology (*Digital worlds*). Among the essays, in addition to those already mentioned above, it is worth mentioning: *Iconography and Electronics upon a Generic Architecture. A View from the Drafting Room* by Robert Venturi (MIT Press, Boston 1997); *City of Bits* by William Mitchell (MIT Press, Boston 1996); *Cybercities* by Christine Boyer (Princeton Architectural Press, New York 1996). But in these magazines and critical essays, one concept is never clearly expressed that now appears certain, namely that, after years of interregnum marked by mannerist wanderings, traditionalist nostalgia and nihilist masochism, computer architecture has replaced that of the machine age, namely, the Modern Movement. Computer architecture is not, as some would like it to be, one of the many fashions that characterize the caprices of the modern world, but a phenomenon that works on the long wave, if we can use this adjective to describe the waves of a history that is becoming increasingly accelerated. This explains the refusal to group the protagonists of contemporary architecture under a decon label, a style that will burn itself out – if it has not already done so – within the space of a few years and, instead, the attempt to outline, using three key words – projection, mutation, simulation – a destiny of our culture and, in the last analysis, the structure of our intelligence.

3.7 A new language

The essay by Sergio Lepri appeared in *Teléma*, winter 1996-97.

4. SIMULATION

4.1 The art of memory

The information on the art of memory is taken from the magnificent work by Frances A. Yates, *The Art of Memory* (Routledge & Kegan Paul, London 1966). It is interesting to note that Yates worked at the Warburg Institute, a neo-Kantian stronghold founded on the teaching of Ernst Cassirer and Erwin Panofsky. For the latter, man organized reality using symbolic forms, namely, using mental *a priori* that differed from age to age, and civilization to civilization (cfr. the essay by Erwin Panofsky on this subject entitled, *Perspective as Symbolic Form*, Zoone Books, New York 1991). The boxes of the memory identified by Yates can be interpreted in this sense. It is worth noting that in works like *Discipline and punish* (Vintage Books, New York 1979) and *The order of things* (Vintage Books, New York 1973), Michel Foucault – who can also be defined a neo-Kantian and who has worked in the more elliptical French cultural context – has highlighted the close connection between the structure of the mind and the ways in which space and architecture are organized.

4.2 Jung's interior telescope

The description of Jung's house in Bollingen is taken from his *Ricordi, sogni, rifles-*

sioni (Rizzoli, Milano 1992). For a Jungian reflection on architecture, see the work by Gaston Bachelard and, above all, *La poétique de l'espace* (PUF, Paris 1957).

4.3 A city where no one dies
A good introduction to Arakawa's work is by Arakawa and Madeline Gins, *Architecture: Sites of Reversible Destiny* (Academy Editions, London 1994).

4.4 The labyrinth
The positive interpretation of a labyrinth as the prototype of a hypertext, namely, a work with several dimensions, is flanked by a negative one: the labyrinth as the metaphor for the loss of the center and the impotence of mortal creatures. In *Aleph* (*Aleph and Other Stories*, Dutton, London-New York 1970) Borges compares the labyrinth to the wandering of the Immortals: "I had found my way through a labyrinth, but the shining city of the Immortals frightened and repulsed me. A labyrinth is a building constructed to confuse men; its architecture, abounding in symmetry, is designed for this purpose. In the palace that I explored in haste, the architecture had no purpose."

4.5 Virtual
Moving towards an increasingly complex spatialization of thought, it is important to underline the positive role of many software programs organized as open instruments for the production and creation of new metaphors, namely, new chains of links to organize reality. This will lead – irony of fate – to the fulfilment of a prediction made jokingly by Borges: the construction of a machine for the production of metaphor.

HYPERARCHITECTURE. AFTERWORD BY ANTONINO SAGGIO

The term "HyperArchitecture" has been used in a completely different context (how to "present" and transmit architecture over the Net) in the site http://flux.carleton.ca/SITES/HYPER/Hyper.html, which is nonetheless interesting to visit. Anyone wishing to continue in the analysis of themes concerning the metaphorization of architecture and landscape should refer to the proceedings of the conference held in Modena on the theme "Paesaggismo e linguaggio grado zero dell'architettura," edited by Bruno Zevi, in press.

The photographs reproduced on pages 12, top of 13, 52, 64 and 69 are by Hisao Suzuki. The photographs on pages 32-33 are by Jeff Goldberg/Esto. The Publisher is willing to acknowledge any rights concerning omissions regarding rights to reproduction of photographs and illustrations.

The Information Technology Revolution in Architecture is a new series reflecting on the effects the virtual dimension is having on architects and architecture in general. Each volume will examine a single topic, highlighting the essential aspects and exploring their relevance for the architects of today.

Other titles in this series:

Digital Eisenman
An Office of the Electronic Era
Luca Galofaro
96 pages, 60 color and 80 b/w illustrations
ISBN 3-7643-6094-1

Information Architecture
Basis and Future of CAAD
Gerhard Schmitt
96 pages, 70 color and 40 b/w illustrations
ISBN 3-7643-6092-5

Further titles will be published in the near future.

For our free catalog please contact:

Birkhäuser – Publishers for Architecture
P. O. Box 133, CH 4010 Basel, Switzerland
Tel. ++41-(0)61-205 07 07; Fax ++41-(0)61-205 07 92
e-mail: sales@birkhauser.ch
http://www.birkhauser.ch